HELL
ON
EARTH

HELL
ON
EARTH

Bob Larson

Bob Larson Ministries
Box 36480
Denver, Colorado 80236

International Standard Book Number 0-88419-072-2
Library of Congress Catalog Card Number 73-86953

Contents

	Preface	7
1	Satanism and the Jesus Revolution	11
2	Games People Play	28
3	The Age of Aquarius	57
4	The Sin of Sodom	74
5	Rakashan	104
6	Incubus	126
7	The God of Hellfire	153
8	Finders Keepers	188

Preface

This book was originally published in 1974. At that time, the occult was a major concern in the Christian community. Evangelical books regarding demonic phenomena flooded the market. Then, in the late seventies, the interest in Christian literature concerning the occult faded. Some undoubtedly did have an unhealthy preoccupation with demons. Now, however, the pendulum has swung the other way to a benign recognition of occult practices. Satan certainly hasn't gone away. A quick survey of television programs, movies, and novels will readily confirm this fact. That's why this reprint is so important.

Mr. Larson is currently preparing a revision of this book. In the meantime we are publishing this paperback edition. We recognize that some material in this volume is dated. The Jesus revolution has melded into the Christian mainstream. Certain trends and specific references are no longer applicable (e.g., some of the gay rock groups mentioned). But the remainder of the information has a timeless relevance which makes this book a valuable guide to understanding our Enemy.

The Publishers

About the Author

Bob Larson, musician, author and evangelist, is a young man with an exciting background. He is a former rock entertainer and disc-jockey. Since his conversion to Christ, Bob has written ten books that address issues of contemporary concern. Several major periodicals and newspapers such as NEWSWEEK, THE MIAMI HERALD, THE MILWAUKEE JOURNAL, THE LOS ANGELES TIMES HERALD, THE CHICAGO DAILY NEWS, THE DALLAS TIMES HERALD, THE TAMPA TRIBUNE, and THE DETROIT NEWS have carried feature stories regarding Mr. Larson's ministry. He is much sought after for television and radio interviews.

Bob has visited over seventy different countries of the world and has lectured on two thousand secular campuses. He has produced two documentary films, several television series, and his daily broadcast of provocative commentaries is carried on more than one-hundred-fifty radio stations around the world.

Bob and his wife, Kathy, reside in Denver, Colorado, where he serves as President of Bob Larson Ministries, a non-profit corporation. Most of their time is spent traveling across America and Canada, conducting an extensive schedule of crusade outreaches. His varied talents as a singer, guitarist, and composer of over 200 songs are an added attraction to these efforts. He also has recorded six gospel music albums.

As one who understands the problems facing the man-on-the-street, he is able to convincingly relate current trends to God's Word. His is an interdenominational ministry with an international burden reaching thousands with the Good News.

1

Satanism and the Jesus Revolution

Speculative theology regarding end time spiritual conditions has been of concern to Christians since the first century after Christ. Some have predicted that the latter days would be a time of great spiritual awakening. They reasoned that the New Testament enthusiasm that earned the followers of Christ the reputation of "turning the world upside down" would be duplicated by those in the Church of the last century before Christ's return. Those who foresaw revival in the end time believed that the bride Christ would return for would be victorious and conquering. Joel 2:28 was their keynote, declaring, "And it shall come to pass afterward, that I will pour out of my spirit upon all flesh." They envisioned an end time fervor similar to that on the day of Pentecost that would sweep millions into the Kingdom of God.

Another school of thought pictured an equally contrasting, negative scene. Making reference to scriptural descriptions of a "falling away" at a time when "the elect" would nearly be deceived, their prediction was one of apostasy and lethargy gripping the Church. They quoted I Timothy 4:1, which says, "The spirit speaketh expressly, that in the latter times some shall depart from the faith, giving heed to seducing spirits and doctrines of devils," and insisted that the powers of darkness would overwhelm many, producing compromise and apathy. As a result, they reasoned that Christ would return only to a faithful remnant that remained true in the face of persecution and martyrdom.

We have now entered what I firmly believe to be the final generation before the return of Christ. In the Gospel of Luke, chapter twenty-one, Christ gives two distinct clues. He refers in verse twenty-four to the fact that "Jerusalem shall be trodden down of the Gentiles until the times of the Gentiles be fulfilled." This, I feel, has been fulfilled as a result of the Six Day War in 1967. The second clue in that chapter is found in verses twenty-nine through thirty-two. The parable of the fig tree is universally accepted by Bible scholars as a metaphoric reference to Israel. The dispersion of the Jewish nation has come to an end, and in line with Bible prophecy the Jews have returned to possess their homeland since 1948. With these prophecies in mind, arguments regarding the spiritual condition of the end time can cease. What this decade has shown us is that both of the views discussed were right. The rising interest in

12

occultism and the surging fervor of spiritual zeal among America's youth (journalistically referred to as the "Jesus revolution") indicate that Joel 2:28 and I Timothy 4:1 are merely opposite sides of the same spiritual coin. What we now see is that these final hours before Jesus comes are being characterized by both apostasy and evil as well as a pouring out of God's Spirit upon hungry, earnest lives.

Let me share with you what I see as some of the detriments and assets of the interest in Satanism as well as the growing Jesus movement.

Without denying the validity of the obvious spiritual awakening that is occurring among America's youth, there is much in the Jesus movement that I find disturbing. I criticize not to condemn, but in the hopes that a purification of the movement may take place as the result of conscientious introspection upon the part of those involved in it.

As outlined in my book *Rock and the Church,* I am perhaps most disturbed by the forms of music evangelism that have surfaced in the Jesus movement. I am not referring generally to contemporary sounds but to those groups that chart the far fringes of the hard-rock spectrum to turn on an audience for the sake of physical appeal and entertainment. I have observed several such groups in action and speak from experience as to the affect they may have on an audience. This may sound harsh, but some Christian-rock musicians are using Jesus as a musical frame of reference to ego-trip in front of a crowd and manipulate the groin while professing to appeal to the spirit. Some have been saved such a short time that they are not sufficiently mature in spiritual preception to use the powerfully perceptual medium of music to communicate the gospel. I am not talking about how loud the music may be. I just want Jesus to come through, and if I can't hear what they say for what they play, something is wrong.

It is not that volume is bad; evil is not a matter of decibel level. The only danger of high volume is that the sound may overwhelm the crowd, inducing a sexually exciting and emotionally subjective experience. Such an enveloping of sound may very well touch the soulishness of a person without communicating to the deep things of his spirit. Sometimes it is not even the volume that gets in the way of the words. It can be just the structure of the music itself. If I feel more like sensually gesticulating my body in response to the rhythms than I do worshiping God with my heart, spirit, and mind, then communication is taking place on the wrong basis. Fortunately, it seems as if many Jesus-music promoters have recognized this and there has been a toning down of Jesus movement sounds in recent months. If the movement is to mature, more message and less medium is going to have to come through that God can use for His glory.

A similar concern is my apprehension at the tendency of some Jesus movement promoters to parade across the platform converts with dramatic stories but lacking a time-proven faith. Such an overemphasis that glorifies provocative testimonies may provide little objective spiritual truth. Worst of all, the "straight" kids in the church are left feeling that they would have been better to do a little dope or drop a little acid to get a little attention. As one long-haired convert said to me, "When I left the altar, everyone was all smiles and handshakes for months; yet, my short-haired friend who had led me to Christ received practically no attention from the church and lapsed into unconcern and bitterness."

From a theological standpoint, I also question what Francis Schaeffer calls "form without content." I am referring to those Jesus people factions that emphasize experience-oriented emotion but have little understanding of doctrinal truth. Getting high on the historical Jesus may not be regeneration, and the attrition rate of such groups is so great as to suggest that many never did possess a viable faith in the risen Christ. I am further disturbed by the fact that such experience-oriented Christianity tends to foster an ecumenical spirit based upon external manifestations rather than essential, theological doctrine. Thus, religious differences that in the past were considered important enough to foster a Reformation are now casually dismissed to the extent that many within the Jesus movement are able to believe entirely opposite things on essential matters of doctrine with little attention paid to the fact that such differences might very well determine the nature of one's faith in Christ. Perhaps this is one key to the fact that some theological liberals have not been particularly alarmed by the Jesus revolution. As those in this revolution mature, one can wonder if theological apostates will continue to view them with such sympathy.

Another problem stems from the leadership of the Jesus movement. Some have capitalized on antichurch rhetoric to further alienate their followers from established religious bodies. Others have even cultivated the naivete and immaturity of new believers by stepping into an authority vacuum and providing ego-centered leadership. They are thus followed by adoring converts for whom they become an evangelical Jerry Rubin. While attacking the established churches, these exploiters build their own little kingdoms based upon the free time and energetic zeal of their followers. Increasingly, I see that such factions are becoming personality-oriented rather than Jesus-oriented. Here is where I feel the established churches can play a role by welcoming countercultural converts and teaching them, while at the same time providing stable, corporate leadership.

Finally, I am concerned by the tendency toward "pop" religion that relegates faith to slogans and thinks nothing of equating the hallowed name of Jesus with a Pepsi commercial. Recently I was following a car bearing the bumper sticker, "Honk if you love Jesus." At the next intersection a car pulled in front of me with a sticker reading, "Honk if you like sex." My reply to both was affirmative, but I honked my horn at neither.

The other day I passed a car sporting a sticker reading, "Warning: in case of the Rapture this car will self-destruct." After one look at that junk heap, I almost wondered if perhaps I hadn't already missed the coming of the Lord.

At the Woodstock rock fest, a rock group called Country Joe and the Fish led the half-million youth in what has become infamously known as the F-I-S-H Cheer. This consists of the

16

spelling out of a four-lettered sex verb beginning
with F. The conclusion comes when they all
scream with glee what you can find any idiot having scribbled on a bathroom wall. It was recorded
live on the sound-track album, *Woodstock,* the
biggest money-making record of the year in 1970.
I suppose that after the F-I-S-H, Cheer, the so-
called Jesus cheer was inevitable. The latter consists of the letter-by-letter spelling out of the name
of Jesus with the gusto of football enthusiasm. I
must confess, though, that this certainly is not my
way of acknowledging a name that according to
Paul's letter to the Philippians (2:9,10) causes
angels and devils to bow.

I am not saying that my concern with "pop"
religion is scriptural canon. It may be only my
personal tastes, but biblical truth is for me just too
sacred to flaunt in simplistic, Madison Avenue,
lapel-button style. If you want to wear a lapel but-
ton, do so; just make sure you live it! If you wish
to put an "I love Jesus" sticker next to last year's
dent and this summer's "We Visited Yellowstone"
sticker, go right ahead. At the same time (I add,
tongue-in-cheek) you might as well add a rooftop
neon sign to your house that says, "I'm a Christian." My point is this: "pop" Christianity has got
to end somewhere, and reverence for the name of
Jesus has to begin before your faith is meaningful
to those who already too casually use "Jesus
Christ" as an expression of profane disgust. It may
be that such pious paraphernalia has already introduced too much of a circus atmosphere
into Christianity. It is, after all, by preaching and
not sloganeering that men are to be saved.

The Jesus movement may be likened to the

17

story told in the Gospel of Matthew, chapter twenty-two, verses one through fourteen. Within the boundaries of the Jesus movement, there are many who, as in that story, sit about the table of the Lord. They have all the right buttons and patches, they know all the language, and can readily glow with high-on-Jesus stories. They sing the right songs and do the right yells, but they don't have on the wedding garment of a personal faith in the risen Christ. Theirs is a subjective commitment to the *man* Jesus with no objective knowledge of the crucified life in Christ. In spite of my criticisms of the Jesus movement, I am not overly skeptical regarding its future. Though there is much sifting yet to be done within its ranks, I pray for these young people and leave the judging to God. The Lord Himself shall someday come and bid those without a wedding garment to be cast away. He will then receive unto Himself those Jesus people who have truly learned the secret of the crucified life in Christ.

I likewise have many concerns regarding the dangers of the growing interest in Satanism, and would like to now focus my attention upon that phenomenon.

By the strictest definition, Satanism embodies the direct, overt worship of a personal devil through an array of demonic rituals such as the Black Mass. Yet, by broader consideration, worship of Satan may be constituted by indulging in any occult or parapsychological practice that ultimately leads to satanic bondage. As I Corinthians 10:20 and Revelation 9:20 point out, even the worship of idols is in reality the direct worship

18

of Satan who masquerades behind the inanimate god fashioned by hands. Certainly, any person of the slightest moral perception would not be enticed by the thought of sacrificing a finger to the devil, drinking blood mixed with urine, or engaging in sexual licentiousness on an altar to Satan. Yet, these same individuals, some of them Christians, will indulge in occult practices that are ultimately satanic in nature. I am not as frightened by the dark side of Satan as I am by the danger of some of his less obvious devices. Let me explain a few of them to you.

For example, to suggest that white magic is benevolent in nature is to assume that there are two sides to Satan. It must be plainly understood that the power of both white and black magic has the same derivation. There are but two supernatural powers at work in this world—the power of the Holy Spirit and the power of the unholy spirit; the power of God through Christ and the power of Satan through his demons. Because it does not enlist directly the powers of darkness, white magic gives the appearance of being pious in nature, and this is just an illustration of the scriptural truth that Satan is transformed into "an angel of light". To consult beyond-human spirit-agencies for even beneficial purposes is to deny the ministry of the Holy Spirit and to openly reject God.

There is equal danger in assuming that only a neutral telepathic force exists and that such psychic phenomena constitute no Christian danger. Such extrasensory forms of communication can be superficially harmless if experienced in the form of déjà vu or nonoccult premonition. (The latter may well be an example of heavenly, angelic ministering when experienced by Christians.) But to engage in card reading, play so-called ESP games, to seek to read another's mind, or to transfer thoughts is to open the subconscious to satanic infusion. ESP is not the result of releasing some telepathic force within. It is ultimately a yielding to satanic forces from without that will move within if allowed to.

Christians should strongly protest the occult and parapsychological-oriented television programs and personalities such as Kreskin. The former are instruments to arouse the occult curiosity of youth. Mr. Kreskin, the latter, is a clever charlatan who uses deceit and trickery as well as the help of Satan to promote parlor-room satanism. At the same time parents should be very wary of the many new children's games flooding the market that are based upon occult phenomena.

Since other chapters will deal with such topics as the Ouija board and astrology, I will not deal with them at this point. Before, however, I pass on from this section of the chapter I would like to issue several brief warnings against satanic tools of occultism.

1. Never allow anyone to hypnotize you. Contrary to popular opinion, you can be made to do things against your will if the request is phrased in such a way that you do not perceive its moral objections. At best you are surrendering your conscious mental capabilities and placing yourself in the vulnerable position of susceptibility to suggestion. When I received Christ as Savior,

I surrendered my will to the Holy Spirit. Through prayer and the daily guidance of God's Word, I seek to keep that will surrendered to Him. I will not allow another to violate God's peroga- tive to direct my volition, even though I do recognize the therapeutic benefits of medicinal hypnosis when applied by a Christian physician.

2. Cease recognizing Halloween as a holiday. There are four witch Sabbats in the year, and the major night of their activity falls on Halloween. It is the satanist's night of the year, when they recognize their reincarnated "mighty ones," and is no longer a child's playtime of trick- or-treat. This is not a conviction that I have always held but one that God has impressed upon my heart as the true purpose of Halloween has become increasingly more evident.

3. Never visit a haunted house. I am not speak- ing about the Disneyland variety but those buildings that claim a reputation of spirit residence. Demons do have specific places of abode. Don't laugh about ghosts. There are such creatures—demonic, ectoplasmic manifestations of fallen angels. Oppression can result from even a casual visit to a haunted house.

4. Never visit a fortuneteller. Most of them are fakes and ply their trade only for commercial gain. Many, however, are mediums and converse directly with demonic spirits.

5. Never engage in any form of levitation such as table-lifting or other supposed transferring of mental powers into physical energy. To momen- tarily suspend the gravitational laws of the universe requires a supernatural act. Christ ac- complished this with His ascension, but Satan seeks to duplicate it through unwitting accomplices who for fun and games try to lift chairs or bodies off the floor, extending the bodies on their fingertips toward the ceiling.

There are many other warnings that I could have issued against occult involvement. I felt that these were the most prevalent and often ignorantly involved in among Christian people. I would like to emphasize in view of these warnings that Satan has power, but it is second to God's power. Under no circumstances should any supernatural act be taken lightly. Indeed, Satan in a limited sense has power over nature, mankind, and even animal life. But thank God, the Scriptures declare, "Greater is He that is in you than he that is in the world."

In spite of these apprehensions that I have shared regarding the Jesus revolution and Satanism, I am glad to know that God is in control. In both movements there is much of encouragement.

That statement has undoubtedly raised the eyebrows of some readers. "How," you ask, "can there be anything positive in Satanism?" For one thing, as a result of the influence of Satanism this generation is no longer skeptical of the supernatural. Satanism precludes a belief in a transcendent spiritual power, for it is the promise of such superhuman power that lures its adherents. Faith in the tenets of Satanism is based upon the ability of Satan to supernaturally answer the request of his followers, be it a hex, voodoo curse, or enchantment. Therefore, to speak of a supernaturally risen Lord who heals and can perform miracles is no longer considered preposterous today.

Secondly, Satan at last is being revealed as a personally evil creature. To worship him as a distinct entity precludes that he actually exists and is the specific perpetrator of evil in this universe. The publicity accorded the Manson family and similar such ritualistic killings dissolves the image of Satan as red-tailed and two-horned with a pitchfork. At least this generation knows with whom it is dealing, and people are beginning to see the reality that Satan is alive and well.

Thirdly, the reality of demon spirit-beings is no longer questioned. This, I feel too, is positive. Before the best-selling novel *The Exorcist* and movies such as *Rosemary's Baby* and *The Possession of Joe Delaney,* any mention of demons was usually considered a throwback to medieval fantasies. No more. I have long stressed the demon-possession factor in hard rock music. This subject is covered more explicitly in my book *The Day Music Died.* In past years I first had to prove the existence of demons before I could discuss their purpose of human habitation. Today, I find a receptive ear even in the secular world, which no longer considers talk of demon activity a figment of a fanatic. Now demons can be directly dealt with easier because their validity of existence is more readily accepted by the general public.

Finally, and perhaps most importantly, is the positive fact that at last the battle lines of these end times are clearly drawn. Even the most casual, non-Christian observer can see that the battle for the allegiance of men's souls is not being waged by communism, secularism, behaviorism, materialism, or humanism. These isms have been the active agents of Satan, but for some reason he no longer deems it necessary to disguise himself in their cloak. The Bible in Ephesians 6:12 states, "We wrestle not against flesh and blood, but against principalities, against powers, against the rulers of darkness of this world." This truth today is clearly seen and because of Satanism, men now recognize the source of evil in this universe as coming from a distinctly malignant personality—the devil. Christians, therefore, have the advantage of showing a personal Savior, tempted by a personal devil, and through His personal and vicarious death triumphing over Satan. The personally redemptive nature of the Cross can be seen as the antidote for the personal attack of the enemy of our souls.

In spite of my apprehensions regarding the Jesus movement, I am optimistic about its comprehensive impact. Perhaps its greatest benefit came through the world's most widely read periodical, *Time* magazine. While traveling overseas, I have discovered that *Time* is the tourist's major source of stateside knowledge and has profound influence in international circles. In the summer of 1971, its cover story featured the Jesus revolution with the headline, "Jesus is Coming." In the hellish center of Hinduism, Calcutta, India, I strolled to a nearby sidewalk magazine vendor to pick up my weekly copy of *Time*. Standing there next to a fresh pile of cow dung and a casually lounging Brahman bull (in the downtown, center-city area), I picked up that issue regarding the Jesus revolution and could only say, "Praise God." Whether or not I agree with all that the Jesus movement stands for, these countercultural dropouts that the church had given up on had by their new-found faith so stirred the journalistic mind of America that, from Bombay to Bali, Jesus was front-page news.

Furthermore, the Jesus movement has been like an army of shock troopers to stir the American consciousness with the name of Jesus. Consequently, to speak today of faith in Christ does not necessarily draw derisive glances from the public. There are many things that this movement might have been called, but its reputation has earned the title of *Jesus* revolution.

From my extensive travels, I have concluded that the extent of the movement has been glorified out of proportion. It still remains primarily a West Coast phenomenon with stereotyped versions having cropped up at various inland localities. Its numbers I find grossly exaggerated by the religious and secular press. One might even argue that it is not that more youth are getting saved but that those who are have longer hair and more dramatic conversions than their contemporaries of a decade ago; hence, they cause more of a stir. Whatever has happened, however, has put the name of Jesus back in vogue and stirred a new and agressive militancy of Christian youth. Just as the citizens of Antioch called the members of a budding, first-century sect "Christians" (followers of the Anointed One), so in these last days the world has tacked another label on another movement of rivaling fervor. The press might have used terms like "religious youth movement", "the former drug-users movement", or "the pious long-hairs movement." But because

25

their central emphasis has been upon the atoning work of the Son, they have been called the "Jesus (Savior-Messiah) Movement."

Beyond all optimism I have for the Jesus movement, I am thrilled most that, thanks to youth, eschatology is back in vogue. Certainly there are dangers. Sure, there are overemphases and too many on the prophetic bandwagon. But, thank God that in spite of riots in Detroit and Watts, the leftists and rightists, drugs and witchcraft, "God is dead" and Bishop Pike, Berkeley and the Chicago Seven, there have come forth at least part of a generation who cries "JESUS IS COMING!" Of course, some have been presumptuous, forgetting His command to "occupy" until He comes. Perhaps the complacent Church needed just such a jar to remind it that where its treasure is, there its heart is also. Everywhere I go I encounter young people unencumbered by material attachments who seem to have a communal consciousness that the return of Christ is near.

Should the Lord tarry, the Jesus movement, if it is to survive, must evolve into a more stable, less frivolous, church-related phenomenon. In terms of numbers of adherents, Satanism may yet win the masses of youth. Indeed, it was that same periodical, *Time,* that declared almost a year after the Jesus movement story, "The Occult Revival; Satan Returns." A hooded, satanic priest replaced the picture of Jesus on *Time's* cover.

But, hell shall not prevail against God's Church. His Spirit is moving upon the lives of hungry young people and they are capturing Joel's vision—the vision of a grand day when

26

Christ has returned and Satan the source of Satanism, has been bound, defeated, and consigned to everlasting punishment. Satanism or the Jesus Movement are two options available for the total commitment of one's life. Jesus said in Matthew 12:30, "He that is not with me is against me." I invite you to join the Jesus movement—not of youth, former dopers, or long-hairs alone. I want you to join the Jesus revolution of born-again believers of all ages, who find unity the message of Acts 4:12, "Neither is there salvation in any other: for there is none other name under heaven given among men, whereby we must be saved." There is just *one way,* Jesus Christ, the Son of God.

2

Games People Play

"Go directly to jail. Do not pass Go, do not collect $200." Hardly an adult alive would not recognize these words. Monopoly, the game based upon the fantasy of financial investments, has for several decades captivated the imagination of participants in parlor room diversions.

But the games people play today are of a more serious variety. The popularity of Monopoly has waned and has been replaced by an amazing variety of parapsychological pastimes. These new amusements are not child's play. Though their manufacturers attempt to pass them off as harmless and entertaining diversions, they are one of the latest tools in Satan's occult arsenal. If you haven't been to a dime store or novelty or hobby shop recently to see the latest games, do so. If you are a parent with small children, such a visit is an absolute necessity. I have often supposed myself to be a person of contemporary awareness, yet I confess that I was shocked when I recently walked through a family department store and saw the games that were being promoted and advertised as suitable for even childhood consumption.

In fact, let me save you that trip. A journey through the remainder of this chapter will provide sufficient warning against the occult games that people play.

One of the most popular and certainly one of the most dangerous is called Kabala. This rather esoteric pastime is based upon the ancient cabala, which is, according to Webster, a "system of occult theosophy or mystical interpretation of the Scriptures among Jewish rabbis and certain medieval Christians." The form of cabala that we know today first gave rise in the thirteenth century among the Jews of Western Europe. They were seeking to recapture the essence of their alienated culture by searching Platonic and Pythagorian thought. A system of mystical correspondence by which the initiate could supposedly discern the unknown regarding God and the universe was developed. Palmistry, numerology, and astrology were part of this occult communication. Superstitious elements entered in the picture by means of talismans and amulets against the Evil Eye. Some cabalistic speculations were tied into the Hebrew alphabet, while other elements expressed faith in the supposed magical qualities of words such as *abracadabra*.

Today's modern Kabala game works on a principle that combines several forms of occultism in an Ouija-type spirit consultation. The cabalistic device for divination is a plastic platform approximately eighteen inches long, circular in the middle, with a hemispheric ball attached to the bottom upon which it can rest and "float" in any direction. The players sit opposite each other with the Kabala lengthwise between them. Their fingertips are to be placed on opposite ends, very lightly touching the Kabala. At this point they are told to meditate and open up their psychic abilities. On a spindle in the center of the Kabala is the so-called magic eye, illuminated to shine in the dark. It can rotate 360-degrees, depending upon which way the practioners tilt the Kabala on its hemisphere. The center circle is inscribed at its circumference with the letters of the alphabet, the numbers one through ten, and the words yes and no, much like the Ouija board. On the outside of this inscription there are compartments where tiny tarot cards may be placed. On the edge of the rim the signs of the zodiac are also inscribed. A ridge is molded into the circumference into which a marble is placed and is able to roll in conjunction with the magic eye in any direction according to the tilting of the Kabala.

Once the game begins, the players meditate and pose questions for the Kabala to answer. In doing so they may well open themselves up to demon influence, depending upon the degree of commitment of "faith" that they make toward the undefined forces that influence the Kabala. With their fingertips resting lightly it would be not difficult for demons to tilt the Kabala in any direction, thus directing the magic eye and the marble to the appropriate zodiac sign, letter, number, or tarot card. Each subsequent consultation will reveal yet another card or answer as long as the players wish to consult the Kabala. I have heard some startling stories from teenagers as to their testimony regarding the movement of the Kabala. In the words of one of them, "Both of us determined to hold our hands perfectly still and to not move the Kabala at all. Somehow an unseen force tilted it to answer our questions. We were scared at what it said and put the game away and never used it again."

Another equally dangerous example is Parker Brothers' Prediction Rod. This game comes complete with a set of instructions that constitutes a satanic primer on the occult. It describes the history of divination (which is strictly forbidden in Scripture—see Deuteronomy 18:10 and 2 Kings 17:17) with particular attention paid to rhabdomancy, which is the use of a wand to find objects, minerals, and water.

I am conscious of the fact that denouncing divination rods and water witching will step on the toes of some Christians. Unfortunately, there are born-again believers who have resorted to this pagan practice. The theory of dowsing (water witching) is based upon the fact that the witcher supposedly reacts in his subconscious to slight vibrations from underground streams. These vibrations respond wtih an instinctive muscular action that causes the rod to dip toward the location of water. One might suggest that this is no more unusual than the use of a seismograph, which registers tremors from an earthquake thousands of miles away. But something more than vibrations is obviously involved when modern dowsers find water by merely running a divining rod over a map of the area rather than the actual ground. The Prediction Rod instruction booklet leaves the whole issue open to question, suggesting that ESP may somehow be involved, and tells the player that "the way to come to final conclusions, and have fun doing it is to try the test yourself, thus tuning your inner consciousness to the affairs of the outside world."

The game is engaged in by one participant at a time. The player grasps a curved handle from which is suspended a balanced rod with a point at one end. According to the instructions he then shuffles a set of cards on which zodiac symbols are inscribed. These are placed in an arc over circles drawn on the playing board. Next he is instructed to move the Prediction Rod slowly over the entire board from one end to the other, lowering it gradually but "without conscious control, until it dips so far that it is drawn to one card, thereby confirming psychic attraction by physical means." A series of such maneuvers supposedly reveals the clairvoyant abilities of the player, and a progression of cards divines information regarding love, romance, fate, travel, and other predictions. The total concept of the games involves numerology, fatalism, divination, planetary attraction, and astrology.

It may be argued that with this game, and others like it, autosuggestive muscular reaction has a large role to play in supposedly psychic responses. Such a naturalistic explanation will not suffice entirely, for there could be no explanation, as in the case of Kabala, for the spelling out of a meaningful word when pure random selection would only choose an arbitrary sequence of letters. The Christian viewing such a game should undoubtedly come to the conclusion that this opening up to supposed psychic powers provides an excellent opportunity for Satan to exhibit spiritistic phenomena.

Though other occult games are not rigged, the Parker Brothers who make Prediction Rod give the devil a little bit of a push. One thing the instructions don't tell you is that not only one end of the prediction rod is weighted with a magnet, but also each of the concentric circles upon which the cards are laid have some magnetized metal hidden in the board. Thus the prediction rod will invariably be drawn to one circle or another depending upon the degree of magentic attraction. Since the line of distinction between the naturalistic and the occult is so hazy, it should be obvious that no sincere Christian could conscientiously engage in such potentially satanic entertainment.

Another series of games are based upon telepathic phenomena. The best selling of these is Kreskin's ESP, produced by Milton Bradley. Kreskin is the well-known television personality, part charlatan, part magician, and part psychic. In the instruction booklet, the whole area of psychic power is given great credibility as supposedly issuing from some not-understood inner source. The first page states, "No claims of mystical or supernatural powers are made for the equipment supplied in this game." Several devices

33

are used to supposedly test the extrasensory perception of the player. One of these is the pendulum, a plastic teardrop-shaped object suspended from a chain. This is held by the chain and suspended over the board that is marked with lines indicating no in one direction and yes in the other, meeting at right angles. The player is told to ask a question and then wait for the pendulum to swing in the appropriate direction by which the undefined force answers in the affirmative or the negative. Should it move in a circular manner the response from the pendulum is simply, "I don't know." On another portion of the board the alphabet is printed and the pendulum swings in the proper direction of the letter it wishes to define. Then the pendulum is stopped so it can swing in a new direction, choosing another letter, to progressively spell out the word or words required to answer the question.

What is happening here? Obviously, the natural laws of the universe are being suspended—this is a supernatural act which has as its source of power God or Satan. How does Kreskin explain the matter? He calls it "psychosonics" or "sounds of the mind." The instruction booklet describes it this way: "Our subconscious mind, which holds much more power than we are aware of, expresses itself in the pendulum movements."

The booklet goes on to describe other "fun and games" that the pendulum can be used for. These include an array of clairvoyant phenomena, all of which have a long history in satanic circles. In addition, a deck of cards is provided with a variety of geometric symbols. These are also used for the exploring of ESP powers.

As with all other games of this nature, naturalistic explanations could be in order for a partial indication as to these unusual happenings, but there is undeniably an element of the occult and a consultation with satanic powers. It's important to remember: Satan does not require that he be directly consulted. He'll masquerade under any disguise to exhibit supernatural phenomena, thus playing upon the occult curiosity of those unfamiliar with biblical teaching. Slowly but surely they become entwined until they find themselves openly consorting with demonic powers.

There are many other games that could be described such as the Astral Tarot, which is one of the most overtly occult, based upon the ancient tarot divination. A dime store game called Mystique Astrology allows one by means of an elaborate dial to find out a variety of supposed astrological information. These include "your moon sign," "the real inner you," "your best astro dates and mates," "how to romance other signs in the zodiac," and "your sun sign and how you appear to others." The game is advertised with the come-on, "What fun mystique do-it-yourself astrology can be!" Fun indeed! How tragic it is to realize that children are toying with this ancient demon practice and opening themselves up to satanic infusion.

There are just too many games on the market to mention all. One entitled Seance is advertised on the cover with the appeal that you can even "call up Uncle Ernie from the dead." But none of these games is as widespread, devastating, and satanically binding as is America's number-one selling game—Ouija.

35

In spite of the popularity of the Ouija board I am amazed that in Christian circles there is both an attitude of total ignorance regarding its satanic purposes on one hand, while at the same time there are thousands of Christians who naively seek consultation of its "mystifying oracle." Like all other Parker Brothers games, the Ouija board is made in Salem, Massachusetts. Coincidence? Perhaps not.

The Ouija board is nothing more than a piece of pressed cardboard made to wood-like toughness. Across the front of it are listed the numbers zero through nine, the letters of the alphabet, the words "good," "bye," "yes," and "no." On top of the board the so-called counter is placed. The board itself is situated on the laps of two people facing each other, "lady and gentlemen preferred." The fingers of the participants are to rest lightly on the counter with the least possible pressure, allowing it to move freely over the board. According to the instructions, "questions may be asked, and in from one to five minutes the mysterious message indicator will commence to move, at first slowly, and then faster. As it passes over the Ouija talking board, each letter of a message is received as it appears through the transparent window covered by the message indicator in the counter." The players are admonished to be serious about the whole endeavor and instructed not to have a "frivolous spirit, asking ridiculous questions, laughing over it."

The claims of its makers are incredible. The Ouija talking board supposedly "gives you entertainment you have never experienced. It draws the two people using it into a close com-

panionship and weaves about them a feeling of
mysterious isolation. It surpasses in its unique
results, mind reading, clairvoyance, and second
sight. Loaded with fun, excitement, and thrills
more intense and absorbingly interesting than a
mystery story." Satan advertises his product well.

What is the force behind Ouija? The board has
no power in or of itself, only the power which is
given to it through the demon that becomes
spiritualistically attached to it. A believer who is
living in fellowship with Christ cannot get the
counter on a Ouija board to move. In the first
place, a Christian should never be consulting the
Ouija board, but I have known of Christians
ignorant of its occultism who did so, and those
who were serving Christ could not get the counter
to move. Why? In order for the counter to glide
across the board, the one whose fingertips are
placed upon it must take a metaphysical step of
faith, surrendering himself to whatever he defines
to be the unknown force of the board. At that
moment when faith is exercised, Satan seizes the
opportunity to exhibit this supernatural
phenomenon.

If you were to ask the Ouija board for the
source of its power, it would spell out demons,
devil, Lucifer, Beelzebub, Satan, or something
equivalent. I have discovered this from having
counseled with scores of people who have used the
Ouija board and inquired from it as to the source
of its power. The answer has always been the
same. If you have one, burn it or break it. In doing
so, you might experience what I have seen and
heard. I have known Ouija boards not to burn until they were renounced in the name of Jesus. On

other occasions screams have been heard as the board was consumed in the flames, a cry of anguish from the demon attached to it, knowing that its point of contact with those it has occultly subjected has been lost. I have several close acquaintances who are former satanists and witchcraft initiates. Each began his progressive involvement in occultism by consultation with the Ouija board during the early stages.

The most amazing story that I have ever come across is one in which God allowed me to be the instrument of breaking the satanic hold of the Ouija.

Revelation is the name of my weekly television series that explores various provocative themes of contemporary interest. Various episodes have touched upon occult and parapsychological phenomena. As a result of this series, a large volume of mail crosses my desk each week. I take time to read each inquiry personally, but with so many letters it is difficult to have any one grasp my special attention. I must confess that this was my reaction regarding a letter received some time ago.

Dear Mr. Larson:

Several weeks ago I enjoyed and was greatly impressed while viewing your telecast program.

During this past year my wife and I have also experienced a series of phenomenal communications from the unknown which have been carefully documented as they actually happened. At times, we managed to take photographs for their authenticity.

My purpose in writing to you is to gain a personal interview at your earliest convenience. I am confident that a personal confrontation with you in your Denver offices can prove fulfilling to a vast majority of the populace of our land.

My first reaction was to somewhat casually dismiss the correspondence as perhaps coming from an emotionally unstable mind. Something in the tone of the letter suggested to me, however, that this might be a matter that deserved attention. My reply was that I would be happy to meet with the letter writer (we will henceforth refer to him ficticiously as Mr. Smith) if he should ever be near Denver. I frankly never expected to see the man.

Several weeks later I received a phone call—it was Mr. Smith and he was in Denver. He said that he had driven five hundred miles just to talk with me and wondered how soon he could get an appointment. My immediate analysis was that this man indeed must be a quack of some kind. But, once again, I felt that inner prodding that there must be more to this story than the initial appearances indicated. With a slight degree of apprehension I told Mr. Smith that he could come by and see me at our home later that morning.

When the time for the appointment arrived I was amazed to see a well-dressed businessman in a new automobile pull up in front of our house. He walked into our living room carrying under one arm a Ouija board and under the other arm a large stack of papers that was to prove the major focus of attention for the remainder of the day. We sat down and I asked Mr. Smith to begin by sharing the background information as to how be became involved in these "unusual happenings."

What he proceeded to share is perhaps the most remarkable story that I have ever heard regarding someone being involved in occultism through innocent experimentation. Mr. Smith explained that he was a real estate investor and rancher, and at one time one of the largest landholders in the country. His wife of more than twenty years had passed away, and he began some time later to live in adultery with his secretary. He had never heard of the Ouija board until one night at a party one was used as part of the entertainment games. Out of curiosity his mistress (whom we shall ficticiously refer to as Jean) purchased one for their own personal use. Little did they realize at the time that for the next two years their nearly every movement of every day would be directed and dictated by demonic spirit-messages obtained from the Ouija board.

Seated with the Ouija board at one side and the stack of papers on his other, Mr. Smith hardly looked the part of a spiritualistic medium. His story unfolded with a revelation of progressive, satanic entanglement. The first act of divination that the spirits performed by means of Ouija board messages was that of predicting the birth of his daughter's child. The demon identified itself as the spirit of the baby and said that it would enter into the body of the baby when the child was born and then be replaced by a new spirit-guide, Matthew, named after the apostle of the New Testament. Mr. Smith's daughter, who was unaware of all these happenings, named the newborn child Matthew in confirmation of this spirit's prediction.

After several weeks of consulting the Ouija

board, they would awake in the mornings to find spirit writings on the mirrors, windows, and various appliances of the home. The reader may be tempted to look somewhat askance at such happenings, and I must admit that I too was initially skeptical. When I expressed some doubt as to the validity of his story, Mr. Smith produced a stack of polaroid snapshots that had been taken over a series of months. There, plainly written in letters ranging from two inches to two feet high, were the satanic messages. Though somewhat difficult to read because they were written in an unusual script, the words could be deciphered after a few moments of study.

I was quite interested in knowing more about the spirit writings that appeared. The first one they saw was on a small mirror. Another was on the underside of a toilet lid. Mr. Smith showed me the picture, and I read the words, "God is Love." I chuckled slightly at such a ridiculous statement in such an unseeming place and asked why the spirit had chosen such a location to communicate. The explanation Mr. Smith offered was that Matthew wanted to make sure that his messages would be seen and that he could be certain this was one place that would be visited on at least several occasions during the day!

Whenever there would be a period of time in which they would not consult the Ouija board, invaribly the word "talk" would appear scribbled on the wall. The writings appeared to be in a chalklike substance, in white when appearing on a dark object or black on a light object. The messages were never removed but just disappeared when the spirits had achieved their purpose. One message was left on for six weeks. It declared, "Be not a deserter unto God." On another occasion a writing disappeared immediately after a fight with Jean. By this, Matthew expressed his displeasure at any estrangement in their relationship thus hindering their occult communicative powers. One writing that was on a toilet lid would not come off. Jean tried using steel wool to remove the message but eventually had to buy a whole new lid.

When Jean's daughter by a former marriage was about to commit suicide, the spirit said through the wall writings, "Talk to me." Matthew revealed what was about to transpire. They called the girl, and she was in tears near suicide. On another occasion the spirit simply wrote, "Vengeance is mine." There seemed to be no particular pattern to these messages, only a rather chaotic form of communication apparently intended to confuse.

It was at this time that they began to hear knockings about the house. Matthew said that Mr. Smith had been drawn back to this ranch. Several times he had lived here before, but this time there was a special spiritual intent in his return. He was to take all of his wealth and build a temple on the ranch—a "temple of the Holy Spirit" to establish a religion for the hippies of the world.

"I thought that this would be a great thing, because the hippies really need straightening out," Mr. Smith said. "I began to feel that I was a privileged, chosen servant of God to bring about His wonderful purposes."

When Mr. Smith became concerned that he had no religious background at all and had never attended church since childhood, the spirits indicated that they would direct the entire project. It was at this point that he turned to the stack of papers lying at his side. He took them out of the folder and showed them to me. It was a manuscript, single-spaced, typed, and about four inches thick.

"These are the message that came from the spirits," he said. "Jean would sit down at the typewriter and the spirit would just control her fingers. She didn't know what was happening; she just typed, and her fingers would fly across the typewriter. She could talk or do other things while she was typing because it required no active concentration."

Even recounting the story, there was an obvious degree of excitement that gripped Mr. Smith. "I'd never heard about his sort of thing before. Some people thought I was crazy. It scared Jean and she thought it might be a work of the devil."

Mr. Smith went on to tell me that he became so desperate at this point that he went to see a minister. The reverend told him, "Well, what you've gotten in contact with is either very good or very bad!"

What amazing naivete! Imagine, a minster so ignorant of biblical truth as to suppose that Mr. Smith's phenomena could be anything less than the spiritualistic workings of Satan.

How much better off Mr. Smith would have been had his occult involvement ended there, but it did not. The next happenings were almost beyond imagination. The spirit said one night to turn off the electricity and to light a candle. They did, and at the spirit's direction they stared toward the wall. Suddenly the flame leaped up into the air and a face, unknown to them, appeared on the wall for forty-five minutes. During this time they were made to recite the Lord's Prayer.

"The spirit always seemed godly, and everything he told us to do had sort of a biblical sound to it. In fact, the face we saw that night," Mr. Smith said, "had long hair and looked like someone out of the Bible. We both saw it, but the next day the face was gone."

Mr. Smith went on to describe how the Ouija board worked. "It was so light that it almost fluttered. Most of the time one is supposed to touch the pointer but we didn't have to. It moved without any contact from us. In fact, it moved especially well if we placed the board over the top of a Bible. It just floated about."

He said that the spirit even had a slight sense of humor. One time it told them to take the monocle (a piece of clear plastic over the message indicator hole) out of the counter because it couldn't see. What delight Satan must have had in manipulating his innocent victims with such mundane trivialities.

I inquired as to whether or not the spirit had ever predicted any events that actually took place. Mr. Smith indicated that a business deal with two Jewish men was prophesied just as it later happened.

Mediumistic healing was also introduced. Jean had acquired a strange illness (no doubt spirit-induced) which the doctors were not able to cure. Matthew said that certain types of food could cure her. Following his prescription of eating rice, she was well again in a day. After reading a book on the medium Edgar Cayce, Jean began to consult Matthew about other ailments, and Matthew complied with cures for such things as allergies and poison ivy.

The next spiritualistic happening came as no surprise to me.

"One night," Mr. Smith related, "the spirit told us that if we wanted to see God's blood we should go in the yard and look near the horse trough."

He went on to tell that they went outside and, sure enough, there were large, red globs of "something" lying there. At this point I interrupted Mr. Smith.

"Let me stop your story for a minute and tell you what 'God's blood' was like," I intervened. "It was very thick and sticky, had a terrible smell, and if you touched it, it was probably difficult to get rid of."

Mr. Smith's mouth fell open and he looked at me in surprise. "How did you know that? You're right. I put some of the stuff on a piece of paper. It accidently got on my hands and was impossible to wash it off. In fact for four or five days I just had to wear it off. It smelled terrible. Do you mean that what I saw wasn't God's blood? Has this type of thing happened to people before? Could it be that I am not a special instrument of God to establish a new world religion?"

I laughed slightly and assured Mr. Smith that this was not the case. He had merely been an innocent dupe of Satan. "What you saw was not God's blood. It's a spiritistic substance called ectoplasm. There are various theories as to how demons create ectoplasm," I went on, "but there seems to be no logical explanation for it. It is an occult phenomenon that has been known to spiritualistic mediums for centuries. No, I'm sorry Mr. Smith, you are not a specially chosen servant of God. Unfortunately, Satan has used you as a willing instrument to bring about his purposes."

At this point Mr. Smith found my analysis a little difficult to believe. "I just don't understand," he said. "If the spirits were not of God, why did they try to help me so much? You see, I used to drink alot. Matthew told me to quit and I did. In fact he wanted me to quit drinking so badly that whenever I tried to get a drink of scotch and go back for a second bottle the spirit would turn it blood-red. Why would a demon do that?"

I took great pains explaining to Mr. Smith that Satan's purpose is to enslave us and that at times he will masquerade as "an angel of light." "There are so-called religious devils," I told him. "They try to mock spiritual values and morals and deceive people because of their supposedly religious connotations."

This "religious" devil advised Mr. Smith to marry Jean and no longer live in adultery. But the union was short-lived. Jean, who had been a sweet and gentle companion, developed a bad temper and a vile tongue. At times she would fly into a rage and violently attack him. He pointed to his face and showed us several scars where she had struck him with objects. Once she attempted to stab him with a pair of scissors.

At that point I had no doubts as to why this spiritualistic involvement had taken place. Invariably one who becomes enslaved to occultism has had an hereditary history of some blood relative who had demonic attachments. I had earlier in the conversation asked Mr. Smith for a careful analysis of his parentage and relatives. None, he informed me, to his knowledge had ever been involved in occultism. He did remember, though, that Jean had two aunts who claimed to have lived with spirits for three years. Before their occult involvements, Jean got up in the middle of the night one time and had written a poem. She described how she had been staring at a gleam of light and had claimed to see something in the room that looked like an angel. From that point on she had been changed, and it was shortly later that the Ouija board was purchased. I felt I could be reasonably certain in a diagnosis that this Jean was either demon-possessed or at times severely demonically oppressed.

Divorce for the pair seemed inevitable. Matthew warned them that if the relationship were dissolved they would lose all spiritual contact with him. The spirit further threatened with a prediction of a catastrophe befalling them if he were deserted.

With slow and deliberate speech Mr. Smith described the day that they left their house to go to file for a divorce. "My son knew that we were leaving and was going to come to say good-by. Jean didn't like him and didn't want to see him, so we left the house a little early. We had driven only about a mile when my son caught up with us. We left the house ten minutes before our appointment with him. He arrived a few minutes early and ran after us with the news that our house was ablaze. We turned around and went back to the house and watched it burn to the ground. Everything we had was destroyed in the home, including many other pictures we had taken of these unusual happenings."

During the divorce proceedings Mr. Smith described his relationship with Jean as reasonably amiable. Finally, they decided to get together for one last time with the Ouija board. Matthew had said that he wanted to talk with them for fifteen hours. "I just couldn't see it," Mr. Smith said. "I said no way could we talk that long, because every time we had a consultation with the board we were absolutely drained. I would be completely fatigued afterwards. We knew, however, that this was going to be the last time to get together, so we let Matthew have his say."

We next turned our attention to the stack of paper at Mr. Smith's side. The purpose of having obtained it by "automatic typewriting" was to write a book. It was through this means that the words of Matthew were to spread and help establish the new world religion. Most of the messages had a religious theme. "I'll always be with you both and remain faithful to God and you," Matthew had written. One description was about water on the moon, and another discussed sex and reproduction on other planets. Of particular note was the fact that each message contained a chapter-and-verse reference from the Bible. There were also references to Old Testament characters such as Eli and Samuel. Matthew was undoubtedly a religious demon! In fact on several occasions the Smiths awakened to find an opened Bible lying beside their bed in the morning with Scriptures circled indicating their rule for living for that day. The spirit repeatedly told them to read the Bible, but it was always under his direction with Scriptures misapplied and taken out of context.

Matthew explained the purpose behind all these happenings. Under inspiration Jean had typed, "You are not founders of a new, but an old religion. In the temple you are to build you will have many meditations. It will burst for enlargement within a year. You will explain the unknown to give peace of mind to those searching for truth. Most of your converts will be young people of this karma who are turning to drugs, drink, sex, and perverted sex, who feel unloved and unwanted. We love you and God is love. You have many things to straighten out in your own carnal lives. You must be an example of everyone in your present karma."

"Matthew even spelled out karma for us," Mr. Smith added. "At the time we didn't even know what it was, let alone how to spell it. Later he went on to describe what it is and its relationship to ions, which are some kind of electrical force. In addition to karma, Matthew also told us that reincarnation is a fact."

At that point I interrupted to quote the words of Hebrews 9:27, "And as it is appointed unto man once to die, but after this the judgment...."

"There is no truth in reincarnation," I insisted, going on to explain the true biblical view of death.

Other religious messages were ever more absurd. Mr. Smith was told about Noah and the ark. Matthew claimed that there were really fifteen hundred arks, with one family to each ark. The demon deliberately lied about Scripture, saying

49

that God did not flood the whole world and that God had never harmed any of His many worlds. At that point Matthew went into astrology and asserted that God had made seven worlds and that there were people on other planets. This life is not in our form, Matthew insisted, but these worlds are like ours nonetheless and flying saucers are from these worlds.

Matthew claimed that Mr. Smith had been born twenty-seven times before. "Don't laugh," he said to me, "but Matthew claimed that my spirit was that of King David." Jean was apparently less spiritual. She had been born again only fourteen times.

I went on to read how supposedly every person has a guardian angel. Adam and Eve, Matthew claimed were only one of many such pairs in various parts of the world. Then I read a description of Jesus: "He was tall and slender with delicate features and hands that you don't forget. He wore long nails with the strength of God in each finger. Not a bully or a fighter, and darker than most Jews. He had pale, blue eyes and a reddish cast of hair with a curly, slight beard, not a hairy man."

These spirits seemed to preach a rather universal religion and suggested that one should go to all churches and pray to all gods. It even asserted that animals had a soul and are reincarnated after death. But Roman Catholics came in for a particular vent of anger. This was one of the few times, Mr. Smith said, that Matthew lost his temper. Matthew told them, "The pope is wrong even though he symbolizes the largest Christian church. He thinks that he can forgive sin, but he only counsels with his ear. He gives audience to those of high position, but he's just trying to play the part of God."

We reviewed a few remaining portions of the manuscript, and I probed Mr. Smith for every bit of information that I thought would be helpful in spiritual counsel. "I guess that just about sums it all up," he said. "Now I want to know from you what I have been involved in. When I saw your television program I said to myself, 'That young man has my answer.' I have driven all this way to talk to you. I have complete confidence that your analysis will be correct. Whatever you tell me, I'll do. I just want to know if all of this is evil or good."

I couldn't help but marvel at the wonderful grace of God, how He had reached down to this man so deeply involved with Satan and prompted him to view a television program in a motel room one Sunday morning. Now God had brought him all this distance to see me so that I might share with him the truth and reality of Christ and the Scriptures.

Our conversation had revealed that Mr. Smith was almost totally ignorant regarding the Bible and spiritual matters. So for the next half hour I gave him an elementary lesson in basic theology. Gradually and carefully we went through the Bible from Genesis to Revelation. First of all I shared with him those Scriptures which forbid consultation with "familiar spirits," witchcraft, scorcery, divination, and other passages with reference to occult phenomena. Emphasizing the biblical injunctions against any seeking after unknown knowledge, I pointed out that all of these things hinder our faith and trust in God, the one to whom we must yield our lives. Next, we took a scriptural journey through the plan of salvation outlining clearly man's relationship to God and the purpose of Christ's coming to die for us.

Mr. Smith listened intently with an open mind and heart. Just as in childlike acceptance he had stumbled into occult bondage, so it was that he approached what I told him. There was a difference, though. Fear had filled his mind throughout the period of Ouija board consultation, and he was continually questioning in his mind the source of such power and knowledge. Now it was apparent that a great peace had begun to settle into his mind as I unfolded unto him the meaning of Christ's love.

"Are you willing to renounce all these occult attachments and repent of your seeking after the information obtained from the Ouija board?" I asked. "Furthermore, are you willing to destroy this Ouija board and manuscript and thereby sever all links with the past?"

I could tell that this was going to be a big price for Mr. Smith to pay. He said that there would be no difficulty in ceasing to consult the Ouija board but destroying it would be another matter. Matthew had warned him that if he ever harmed the board he would be dead within two years. Since the manuscript had been laboriously obtained after multiplied hours of contact with the Ouija board it would not be an easy matter to destroy it. He had been told that this manuscript would eventually be printed into a best-selling book to promote his supposedly new world religion.

I pointed out that no danger could come to his life by destroying the Ouija board. This was only an instrument of fear, I explained to him, and one that Satan was using for purposes of intimidation. As long as he could trust in Christ and the protecting power of His blood, Satan would not be able to touch him. I stated that the manuscript was a work of Satan and that in no way should he aid these demonic powers by promoting their efforts through the glorification of a publication. As I now sit writing this chapter, I cannot help but think what an irony it is that the devil has gotten the tables turned on him. In a way, Mr. Smith has gotten his book and the devil has gotten his information out but not in the way that either of them had intended.

"First, I am going to pray for you myself," I explained to Mr. Smith, "and then I am going to ask you to say a sinner's prayer."

I knelt with Mr. Smith in the middle of our living room and placed the Ouija board in front of us. "This time," I said to him, "instead of placing the Ouija board on top of a Bible, let's put a Bible on top of the Ouija board."

I began my prayer by invoking the power of Christ and denouncing the evil spirits that had been attached to the Ouija board and to the life of Mr. Smith. Through the authority in Christ's name I commanded the spirits to entirely loose their hold upon his mind and spirit. Feeling a great sense of peace and victory, I proceeded to lead Mr. Smith in a prayer of confession. What a thrill it was to hear him say each phrase after me with conscious deliberation. There was no doubt that he meant each word. At last, the hold of Satan was being broken.

When we had finished, Mr. Smith looked up. A change had come over his life, and he was now seeking God for the first time. Perhaps more importantly, he had denounced the forces of hell, and no longer could they hold sway over him through spiritual ignorance. He glanced at the Ouija board several times and then finally picked it up and smashed it over his knee. It cracked! What a beautiful sound: the sound of victory over Satan.

"I'm going to get rid of this manuscript, too," he said.

We walked into the family room and there, piece by piece, he wadded up each sheet and threw it into the fireplace. I handed a match to Mr. Smith. "I'm going to let you have the pleasure of starting the fire," I declared.

He smiled and seemed to enjoy his duty. We laughed and thanked God, praising Him for the battle being won as the flames leaped upward. In a few minutes nearly every page of the manuscript was consumed, leaving only a few notes from which this account is taken as a record showing the enslavement that had bound Mr. Smith for so many months.

Later that day, we dined and visited further with Mr. Smith. On into the evening we talked, sharing with him more of our faith in Christ. He drank it all in since we were perhaps the first real Christians he had ever met. What a joy it was to pray with him again and commit his life unto the Lord for keeping.

I would like to emphasize to the reader the purposes for the inclusion of this story. In no way do I want to glorify the works of Satan by bringing undue attention to them. My purpose has been to show the way in which one can through ignorance stumble into league with the devil. Almost every case of occultism I have counseled started in this manner. Satan preys upon spiritual blindness, and a mind that is not filled with God's Word is a prime target for Satan's word. I also want to expose the absurdity with which Satan often communicates. By my relating of various portions of the manuscript the reader was undoubtedly able to see that Satan is not only clever, but at times he seems downright stupid. Such goings-on about sex on the moon are ludicrous! The exposure of how Mr. Smith was kept preoccupied with ridiculous and mundane information shows the difference between the communication of Satan and the communication of God through His Word, which is based upon ultimate truth. Finally, I wanted to show the extent to which Satan will use and distort God's Word for his own purposes. Some feel that the devil only approaches people with evil and debauchery. This is not always the case. As in the instance of Mr. Smith, he often masquerades under a religious disguise, using Scripture incorrectly as well as out of context. Don't be deceived by someone or something just because the Bible is used or promoted. Distortion of Scripture has always been a primary tool of Satan.

If you, the reader, have a Ouija board or any other occult game, I am sure your course of action should be well defined. Harboring such an item after having read this chapter could well be not only a foolish but also a spiritually fatal decision.

Destroy the games of Satan, renounce your involvement, and plead the blood of Jesus over your life. If you have not repented of your sins and confessed Christ as your personal Savior, do so now. Remember, it was not a game Jesus played when he left the throne of glory to die for you and for me. Don't reject His love by consulting hell through one of the occult games that people play.

3

The Age of Aquarius

You are very changeable and fickle; you love to experiment.   Love, sex, and everything romantic come to you first as purely mental things. You like to play a thing around in your mind and create fantasies, performing assorted erotic techniques with a partner of the opposite sex long before contact has actually been made. One day you will groove with somebody and the next day you won't; it is as simple as that. Added to all these, you can be in love with several people at once—two would be your usual minimum quota.

Sound like anyone you know? It is supposed to be me, or so says a page from a book entitled *Astrology for Lovers*. The description is found under those whose sign is Gemini. How do I know what my sign is? A minister's wife once told me after she had approached me with the question, "When is your birthday?" Anybody who would ask me that today is likely to get the sermon you are about to read.

Astrology, along with palmistry, witchcraft, numerology, and other forms of occultism, has always interested a few, but today a fad has turned into a phenomenon. Right now there are three times as many astrologers as there are clergymen in the Roman Catholic church. Nearly two thousand newspapers carry a daily horoscope, and there are astrology guides for everything from horse racing to alcoholic drink mixology.

Outside the United States, governmental leaders often openly consort with the occult. Argentina's Peron maintains a personal astrologer, and in Cambodia the advice of astrologers often determines whether armies advance, governments fall, or prime ministers take trips.

In the nineteenth chapter of the Acts of the Apostles in the Bible, a revival in Ephesus resulted in a bonfire in which various forms of occult arts and books were destroyed by converts. My crusades are often climaxed in the same manner. After speaking on the occult I am amazed to see the mass of paraphernalia turned in for destruction by those to whom the Spirit of God has spoken by conviction. It is quite obvious to me that, unfortunately, many Bible-believing Christians are victims of occultism. The most prevalent occult involvement of all is astrology. The book quoted from above was turned in by a Christian teen-ager.

Does astrology work? Is it a harmless pastime? Is there anything wrong with casually consulting one's daily horoscope? What does the Bible say about astrology? These are some of the questions I am going to answer in this chapter.

"I believe we've had a problem here" was the understatement of the space age. With that declaration astronaut James Lovell announced the beginning of a tense human drama that tranformed Apollo 13 from a routine moon flight into four days of peril. Suddenly, a divided world accustomed to suffering and the horrors of violent death shared a common concern for the lives and safety of America's three astronauts. Television networks estimated that perhaps the largest viewing audience in history watched their return.

The astronauts of Apollo 13 had followed the custom of earlier flights by taking along a tape recorder, complete with prerecorded music, to listen to during the long hours in outer space. Just before the explosion that aborted Apollo 13 by tearing a hole in the command module, the astronauts had played a tape-recorded song for mission control in Houston. Ironically, the song they played, "The Age of Aquarius," proved to be coincidentally prophetic. Little did the astronauts know at that time that "Aquarius," their lunar module by nickname, would be their only hope of surviving death from being marooned in outer space. Hours later they were to learn that their lives would depend upon the life-support system and rockets of "Aquarius."

After the safe return of the flight to earth, millions marveled at the ingenuity and adaptability that the space team had exhibited, turning disaster into triumph. Maneuvers and calculations necessary to return the crippled moonship safely required perhaps an even greater degree of proficiency than the first lunar landing. The genius and scientific knowledge of man had seemingly accomplished the impossible.

There is an irony to this dramatic and memorable event. Many Americans watching the return flight reports on television probably glanced intermittently at the newspaper accounts of the voyage. Some making their plans for that day may have well turned to the astrology section of the newspaper to consult their daily horoscopes.

At the same time many teen-agers had in their record libraries the same recording of the song the astronauts had played, "The Age of Aquarius." In July of 1969, when man first stepped onto the moon, this song was the number-one song in the nation, the spot it held for nearly six weeks. In fact, it was voted the pop song of that year and has since become a pop music classic. Nearly every major recording artist has released a rendition of this song.

The lyrics to "The Age of Aquarius" declare: "When the moon is in the seventh house/and Jupiter aligns with Mars / then peace will guide the planets / and love will steer the stars / This is the dawning of the age of Aquarius." The song was taken from the Broadway musical *Hair*. That production had an astrologer listed in the cast, and the opening performance of each production was gauged in conjunction with astrological advice.

Think of it! Man conquers the moon and steps

to the stars. Yet, many on earth still adhere to that ancient notion that the alignment of the planets and the stars and sun somehow control the affairs of men on earth.

It was over fifty centuries ago that the Chaldeans of the Babylonian empire observed the influence of the sun upon the earth and the moon upon the seas. They concluded that the planets were gods and therefore certain conjunctions of their movements would affect wars, governments, and the destinies of men. There were other methods of fortunetelling, such as surveying the entrails of animals, but these often proved unpredictable. At least, the stars were dependable.

Many ancient monuments were attempts to link by astro-alignment men on earth with the gods in the sky. Examples may be found all over the world such as Stonehenge, the Egyptian Nile temple built for Amon-Ra, an extinct Indian city-temple complex near Saint Louis, and Mayan civilization centers. In later centuries, astrology invaded Europe through the Arabs who conquered Spain. They introduced celestial medicine which used astrological predictions for therapeutic ends by suggesting different parts of the body were influenced by certain signs of the zodiac.

How amazing it is that such a pagan conception could hold sway in an enlightened age such as ours.

The recent voyages to the moon are the result of the scientific method which began in the sixteenth century among men who were Christians. They reasoned that the universe was the work of an intelligent Creator and therefore would be orderly and worthy of investigation. It is this

61

basis of thought which has led America to be first to the moon. But our current interest in astrology is a worship of the creation rather than the Creator. In the Bible, the first chapter of Romans speaks of those who changed the truth of God to a lie and "worshipped and served the creation more than the Creator." The judgment of them was such that God gave them to vile affections, sins of perversion, and a reprobate mind. That chapter in God's Word is not only the denunciation of an ancient pagan civilization, but it is also a pronouncement of judgment against America today. "In God We Trust," we say on our coins, but some will not take a step without first consulting their horoscope. Surely, we are on our way to being "given up" by God.

Before going any further it might be well to take a moment and explain how astrology works. I am amazed that even those people who are interested in this occult art seldom understand what it is all about.

Imagine, if you will, a spoked wheel. Envision the center where the spokes meet as indicating the location of the earth and the outer rim signifying the path that the sun takes through the heavens each day as it revolved about the earth. The area indicated by the outer rim is, according to the astrologers, about sixteen degrees wide and represents the zone of the zodiac. What concerns astrologers are the star constellations that appear within this certain band that represents the path of the sun through the heavens. The rim should be divided into twelve equal sections representing the twelve divisions or "houses" of the astrological zodiac. During the course of a year the twelve constellations, or signs of the zodiac, move through each of the twelve houses. In addition, each of the nine planets as well as the moon and sun move through each house every twenty-four hours. There are many other constellations besides these twelve and just why the ancients did not take them into account isn't certain. This does point out one of the fallacies of this pseudo-science. It may be that they reasoned the sun's rays would have to shine through the constellation to affect the people on the earth below (indicated by the earth at the center of the spokes). In determining one's horoscope the exact geographical spot of one's birthplace is coordinated with the date and hour of birth. The conjunctions and relative positions of all heavenly bodies are considered by the angles they form with relationship to each other. From this information the horoscope is eventually computed.

There are several problems raised by this simplified illustration of how astrology works. The major one is that the entire illustration is completely without purpose. Astrology originated in the pre-Copernican age when the earth was thought to be the center of the universe. We know now that in reality the sun does not circle the earth but vice versa. Because astrology is based upon an erroneous concept of the universe (the sun circling the earth), its suppositions and conclusions are therefore completely without any scientific basis. There is no relationship whatsoever to any real science.

Other problems are raised as well. The sun has an uneven wobble as it spins on its axis and thus there has been a shift in the zodiac. In reality the rays of the sun today enter each of the constellations about one month earlier than they did centuries ago when the present astrological charts were finalized. This means that one's horoscope reading is in reality off one complete sign. Even if the predictions of astrology were true, they would not be applicable by an error of one month.

A new book by an astrologer entitled *Astrology Fourteen* asserts that there are actually fourteen constellations in the astrological zodiac. If the predictions of astrology were to be correct scientifically, these two extra constellations would have to be included as well. Furthermore there are some people born without a horoscope. What about those who live north of the Arctic Circle? No planet assigned to the zodiac is visible there for several weeks out of the year. Does this mean that Eskimos and Norwegians have no celestial influences upon their lives and thus no astral destinies?

No one really knows for sure who had the right astrology. As I have traveled through different parts of the world I have recognized that astrology is a universal, pagan practice. But no two religions agree on the proper horoscope readings for each sign or astral view of the constellations. If you were to have your horoscope computed by a Hindu in India it would read much different than that of a Buddhist in Bangkok. The difference between characteristics delineated by certain planets raises another question. Who is to say whether Mars is good or bad and who a certain relationship of one or more planets should portend good or evil fortune?

Consult an astrologer and he will make a great deal out of the exact moment of birth in relationship to heavenly bodies. But who today determines when a child is born? Certainly not Mother Nature. More often the doctor decides the hour and date of birth for family and hospitalization convenience. Would it then be possible for a physician to thwart one's astrological destiny by manipulating the moment when the fetus emerges?

Astronomers, those who engage in the true science of stargazing, completely reject astrology, relegating it to the ranks of superstition. Yet there are millions of people who waste multiplied hours and countless dollars studying signs of horoscopes which tell them absolutely nothing about themselves except what they read into them, which most generally is of a complimentary nature. If this were all there were to astrology we could simply laugh it off as so much foolishness, but because it is a way of life and religion for millions of people, and has been throughout recorded history, we must address ourselves to how and why its predictions do come true and look as well at the biblical views of this pagan pseudoscience.

Can celestial bodies influence the lives of people on earth? Certainly not, according to the precepts of astrology. There is a way in which the widely held philosophy of astral influence may possibly be explained. Have you ever gazed into the heavens and wondered what the reason could be for the existence of what astronomers tell us are billions of stars at incomprehensible distances? God is not a purposeless Creator. Perhaps these bodies are for more than the declaration of God's awe and majesty. Someday, in our redeemed state, intergalactic travel and communication may be possible. Thus, the stars may be within the realm of our habitation. The Bible also teaches that the universe is the scene of invisible warfare between the forces of God and the "principalities and powers, and rulers of darkness." The book of Daniel clearly illustrates this fact. Since Satan is the "prince of the power of the air" (Ephesians 2:2) it may be that the stars are somehow involved in this cosmic struggle. Though the physical mass of the stars can have no affect upon the lives of earthly men, the demonic spirits connected with them might somehow work in such a manner. Such a theory is entirely speculative, as no clear biblical teaching can convincingly be found in such matters.

More often the "correct" predictions of horoscopes can be attributed not to what Satan knows in the future, but to what he plans to do in the future. Satan does not know the future; that alone is God's knowledge. He is the one who knows and holds tomorrow. Satan can, however, with extreme accuracy, discern the future by consulting God's Word and perceptively viewing events and circumstances.

Here is what may happen when a person reads his horoscope. The moment a horoscope is read, Satan employs his most effective tool: the power of suggestion. The reading of a horoscope plants in the mind the possibility of a certain happening. Immediately, Satan (through his spirit-demon agencies) begins to work behind the scenes to structure events that will eventually fulfill what the horoscope predicted. Then, if he is successful and the prediction comes true, you may find yourself saying, "Isn't that amazing, the horoscope knew my future!" No, my friend, the horoscope did not know the future. Satan only committed himself to a certain prediction and then by the power of suggestion sought to have that prediction fulfilled so that you would think it was actually the foreknowledge of the horoscope, when all along it was only the progressive influence of Satan upon your life.

Let us look for a moment at the biblical response to the occult practice of astrology. The first reference to astrology in the Bible is in the eleventh chapter of Genesis. Here we find the story of the building of the tower of Babel. Archaeologists have now discovered that the tower of Babel and similar towers were actually ziggurats which the early Chaldeans erected to survey the heavens. Some ziggurats that have been unearthed contained zodiacs inscribed on the circumference of the top. The Bible says that the purpose of the tower of Babel was to have a tower "whose top may reach unto heaven." The Chaldeans were not simple and ignorant but a highly advanced civilization. They had sense enough to know that it was not literally possible to build a tower that could reach heaven. This phrase may well be a biblical metaphor that could be better translated a tower "whose top may be used to reach out unto the heavens." There is little doubt its real purpose was to survey the stars for astrological purposes.

Because these men sought to discover their destiny in the stars rather than communicate with God, judgment was brought upon them. Confusion and division was the result. As we look about us in America today we see much perplexity and distress in modern life. Could this be the result of God's judgment bringing confusion upon our land for pursuing the ancient, pagan practice of astrology?

There are numerous other biblical references to astrology. One is found in Isaiah 47:13-15. Here the Babylonian astrologers were mocked by the prophet of God for following such a superstitious practice. God's word not only condemns astrology but ridicules it as well, holding it up to be a very vain thing in which to trust for one's salvation.

Those who consult astrology are anxious and fretful about the future. Jesus said in Matthew 6:25 that we should "take no thought" for our lives. He declared that the necessities of life would be provided by our heavenly Father if we would seek Him first. It is not ours to know what shall be on the morrow but to face tomorrow with the help of God. We may not know the future but we can know one who holds the future. We must be willing and able to trust Him to guide us through each day. This is faith. Astrology is a crutch.

The next time someone asks you what your sign is, quote unto them the words of Jesus in Matthew 12:39, "An evil and adulterous generation seeketh after a sign." To seek to know the sign under which one is born is to deny the sign of our Savior's life, His death, burial, and resurrection.

In Psalm 19:1 we read the following words:

"The heavens declare the glory of God; and the firmament showeth his handiwork." The emphasis of astrology is upon nature rather than the God of nature. From this psalm we see that the purpose of the heavens is to declare the glory of God, not the destinies of men.

The underlying philosophy of astrology is that our destinies can be found in the stars. The supreme tenet for the Christian faith is based upon the attitude that individual moral decisions and the exercise of our free will determine our destinies. Astrology attempts to destroy man's personal moral responsibility. He can always fall back on blaming the stars for, after all, it is really their fault. Remember, this is a lie. Some day we will each stand accountable before God (Romans 14:12). God will not hear some lame excuse that our stars and planets were in the wrong conjunction and therefore we weren't responsible for what we did.

The Bible is clear in denouncing astrology. In Jeremiah 10:2 we read, "Learn not the way of the heathen, and be not dismayed at the signs of heaven; for the heathen are dismayed at them." The prophet goes on to equate astrology with idolatry and describes the vain way in which the heathen seek to please and follow their astrological gods. He concludes by saying in verse six, "There is none like unto thee, O Lord."

The clearest command against astrology is found in Deuteronomy 18, beginning with verse nine. As the children of Israel are about to enter the Promised Land, God issues severe warnings against the practices of the heathen in those nations. One such warning is against any Israelite becoming an "observer of times," which is an astrologer. This practice, God declares, is "an abonimation unto the Lord." The penalty for its practice was death by stoning. Let it be said clearly and plainly: to indulge in the practice of astrology, even the casual consulting of one's daily horoscope, is to act contrary to one of the most solemn warnings of Scripture. Astrology is in direct disobedience to almighty God. Those who practice it expose themselves to the wrath and judgment of God.

Thus, you see, there are many reasons for rejecting this ancient pseudoscience, but the supreme reason for dismissing the occultism of astrology is its erroneous predictions of the future.

"This is the dawning of the age of Aquarius / harmony and understanding / sympathy and trust abounding"—this is the lyrical proclamation of the hit song "The Age of Aquarius." What is the age of Aquarius? Much as we Christians theologically divide periods of history into dispensations, astrology also divides history into time periods. Astrologers say that once every 26,000 years the equinoxes occur in their original positions. Since there are twelve houses in the zodiac, dividing twelve into 26,000 yields 2,200. This time period of 2,200 years is called a star age. The beginning of a star age is indicated on the day in which the sun rises on the first day of spring in the space occupied by that particular sign of the zodiac. For the last 2,200 years this has occurred in the space occupied by Pisces, the sign of the fish. The age of Pisces has supposedly been an age of death, tears, and sorrow. The age of Pisces, according to astrologers, has been an era marked by skepticism and pessimissim. The astrological theory has it that about 1904 we entered a new star age, the age of Aquarius. The age of Aquarius is supposed to signify a period of new spiritual beginnings with promise of new universal brotherhood, freedom of expression, and the shedding of inhibitions. Thus we see that the song "The Age of Aquarius" is not only an expression of those ideals youth hope to achieve in our society, but it is an astrological prediction of the future. This, however, is where astrology falls entirely short.

Far from facing an optimistic age of harmony and understanding, the biblical view of the future is sober and filled with devastating prophecies. Revelation 6:6 predicts a famine unlike any ever known on earth, and the twelfth through fourteenth verses of that chapter predict a gigantic earthquake, the sun becoming black, the moon appearing as blood, and stars falling while mountains and islands are moved about. Revelation 8:7-12 says that one-third of the trees on earth will be burned and one-third of the sea life destroyed. A horrible pestilence of scorpions and locusts is described in Revelation 9 as plaguing the earth for a period of five months. Even more terrible events are described in Revelation 16. There we read that the rivers and waters of earth shall become as blood, the sun will give forth such intense heat that men will be scorched and gnaw their tongues from pain, and hailstones, some weighing as much as 100 pounds, will fall from the heavens. What a far cry this is from the age of Aquarius that astrologers would have us to believe lies just around the corner.

There is a way out. You, my friend, do not have to go through these horrible events which I have just described. Immediately preceding the fulfillment of these prophecies the blessed hope of the ages shall take place, the translation of the church. In I Thessalonians 4:16,17 and I Corinthians 15:51,52 the apostle Paul spoke of how those who know Christ as Savior shall rise to meet with Him in the air and from that time on dwell with Him forever. Those who have been redeemed by the blood of Christ shall not have to face the consequences of the prophecies of Revelation. While these events are unfolding on earth, the saints of God shall be enjoying a grand reunion with their Lord and Savior.

But if you are looking for an age of harmony and understanding, with sympathy and trust abounding, let me assure you that God has prepared just such an age. It's called the millennium, the one-thousand-year rule and reign of Christ that will be established here on earth immediately following the horrible events predicted in Revelation. The millennium, "God's age of Aquarius," will surpass anything the songwriters could ever have dreamed of. Universal love, peace, and brotherhood are terms inadequate to describe the state of men on earth during that time. The prophet Isaiah gave a clear description of this age. So wonderful will that time be that he declared that in those days men would "beat their swords into plowshares and their spears into pruninghooks" and that they would "learn war no more." The peace of God shall so fill the earth that "the wolf also shall dwell with the lamb, and the leopard shall lay down with the kid;

and a little child shall lead them."

The age of Aquarius is a diabolical lie, a satanic counterfeit. You may prepare for its supposed reign of peace and understanding, but I am preparing for the return of Jesus Christ.

Your fate is not in the stars. Your future and eternal destiny will be determined by the exercise of your will and the choice you make as to what you will do with Christ who gave His life for you. We are not living on the dawning of a new age, but we are nearing the close of the final age. This age will be terminated by the return of Christ in the clouds of the air to receive those who have trusted in Him as Savior. Will you be ready?

4

The Sin of Sodom

If you get into a cab in New York and ask the driver to take you to the Great Northern Hotel on West 56th Street, you are likely to get an unusual look. He probably knows that your destination is not for overnight accommodations. More than likely you are headed for the Continental Baths. The Continental Baths is one of the many new homosexual spas cropping up across the country, where all anybody wears is a towel and the worst forms of perversion are allowed and encouraged. The older, gay "steam baths" were operated like bars during Prohibition. Most were rather clandestine, and the only way you could get there was to find the address from a friend. Upon arrival, you had to convince the proprietor that you

74

were a homosexual and sign a ficticious name to the club roster. Once inside, a dark and dingy atmosphere greeted the customer.

The Continental Baths, opened in September of 1968, changed all that. Inside, the Continental is like a luxurious health spa with private rooms for homosexual relations and a large open dormitory with bunk beds and a floor full of pillows. This is the so-called "orgy room" where ten to thirty men may be making contact at one time. Other attractions are a snack bar, a jukebox, a dance floor, and a performing stage where name entertainment artists come. The proprietor, a homosexual himself, says that it is not unusual for a man to spend his entire weekend there, coming in on Friday night and staying until he goes to work on Monday. Some nights there may be fourteen hundred customers there at once. Even some nonhomosexuals have come to attend the floor show. One such recent visitor, Mick Jagger of the Rolling Stones, had to leave rather abruptly when, due to his reputation for bisexuality, he was approached by several young men who promptly dropped their towels.

I have seen the Baths of Caracalla in Rome. Today these baths are in crumbling ruin and have been transformed into an outdoor stage area where summertime drama is portrayed. The history books will tell you the Baths of Caracalla were for communal cleanliness, but those who know the other side of Roman history are aware that much more than that went on there. Standing by these ruins I could not help but think that they were mute testimony to that pagan civilization so given to perversion that its population actually declined during its final years of existence.

While some may read the first chapter of Romans in the Bible and suggest that God is going to judge America for the current surge of perversion and gay liberation, I think that may be getting the cart before the horse. What Romans 1 actually tells us is that the sin of Sodom is an evidence that God's judgment has already been visited upon a civilization. This sin is evident when a nation has *already* turned its back on God. America will not only be judged for perversion; perversion is America's judgment.

I would rather not write on this subject, and perhaps many of you are already convinced that I have been too explicit in this brief beginning. Yet if I am to preach all of God's Word I cannot ignore His warning against this growing evil. The apostle Paul wrote to the Ephesians, who lived in a city given over to the most depraved religious practices. He reproved them by declaring in Ephesians 5:12, "It is a shame even to speak of those things which are done of them in secret." You may feel that it is better for me not to write about this subject and may quote this Scripture as the basis for your objection; yet our situation is much different from that of the Ephesians. Those things of which Paul spoke are no longer done in secret but today are practiced openly. It therefore is no longer a shame to speak of those things but rather an imperative necessity, considering the fact that many today do not understand the biblical basis for God's disapproval of homosexuality. This urgency was certainly underscored by the Houston homosexual slaying—twenty-seven young men assaulted and murdered by a pervert whom police officials said "must have been a madman."

The homosexual is no longer a whispered-about suspect but an agressive defender of his perversion. What was once spoken of in shame by even the most blatant of sinners is today proclaimed in marches and demonstrations. Arm in arm they chant, "Two, four, six, eight, gay is just as good as straight." The sin of Sodom is no longer a carefully guarded private secret but a matter of personal pride.

As America has grown increasingly permissive in sexual matters, the homosexual has felt less threatened and repressed in his deviance. Consequently, a writer for the *New York Times* has proclaimed his homosexuality and a District of Columbia congressional candidate ran on a platform demanding homosexual rights. The new sheriff of San Fransisco openly credits the city's homosexuals for his victory margin. An Army WAC has married another female soldier, and folksinger Joan Baez claims to have "doubled her pleasure" with bisexuality. A homosexual magazine even advertises tourist junkets for "people interested in meeting those with similar interest." And now some judges have even ruled in favor of acknowledged lesbian mothers!

With numbers estimated from two to twenty million, deviants represent a powerful minority force proclaiming, "Gay is good." More visible than ever before, homosexual organizations can be found in every large city and on many college campuses. They are militant in defense of their life-style, and they picket, testify at government hearings, appear on television shows, and even organize their own churches. Most importantly, they no longer hide their identities but publicly reveal their names and freely discuss their lives and "lovers." Others have joined the "oldest profession" and offer their services for as much as $100 a trick. "Chickens," as they are known, are usually young, but a significant portion are from upper-middle-class families, seeking a secret moment of sexual release in a cheap motel room.

Lavender Panthers is the name of the new gay vigilante organization formed to protect their confreres from attacks. They patrol the streets under the leadership of former evangelist Ray Broshears, who says, "If there was such a thing, I'd work with the devil to bring about gay rights." Make no mistake about it, homosexuals represent the largest minority social protest movement in America.

As might be expected, rock music has been in the forefront of Satan's attack on the sexual values of America. Indeed, rock has encouraged perversion and is a keen barometer of its involvement among those in the counterculture. Some rock promoters are predicting that the major trend for this decade is going to be called Gay Rock. While some artists have softened their sound and turned to themes of love, others are pushing in an extreme and sometimes unsavory direction. Certain rock stars are taking a new interest in exploring themes of homosexuality and transvestitism. Complete with ultra-high-heeled shoes, shoulder purses, and women's clothing, they take the stage to publicly flaunt their perversion.

With the unisexual fashions in full swing and women now wearing man-tailored jackets, ties, and fly-front trousers, it was only a matter of time before fingernail polish, lipstick, and make-up would become part of a male performer's wardrobe. Today you don't know whether a rock entertainer is going to walk out on stage with a guitar or a purse. Rock groups that used to pass around a joint before their performance now pass around the Max Factor. Their condemnation is explicitly described by the apostle Paul in I Corinthians 6:9,10. There Paul states that those who are "effeminate" shall not inherit the Kingdom of God. The display of perversion through the wearing of female garments is prohibited and condemned as well in Deuteronomy 22:5, where it is stated, "The woman shall not wear that which pertaineth unto a man, neither shall a man put on a woman's garment: for all that do so are abomination under the Lord thy God." This passage does not refer to clothing only but to anything peculiar to each sex which clearly and unmistakably distinguishes it from the other. There can be no doubt that the gay rock groups who cross sexual lines of distinction in clothing come under God's judgment.

The rock interest in homosexuality is not entirely recent in origin. Several years ago the Kinks took a fling at homosexuality and sexual ambiguity with a song called "Lola" declaring, "She walked like a woman and talked like a man." The leader of the group, who wrote the song, Ray Davies, often deliberately gives a homosexually oriented performance. In like manner Frank Zappa and the Mothers of Invention were exploring bisexual themes as early as the mid-sixties. For the cover of one album they were pictured in women's clothing.

Various artists have recently gotten into the homosexual bag. Keith Moon of the Who frequently appears in public in women's clothing. Mark Bolan of T. Rex. often wears make-up and flaunts a deliberately bisexual image. Another group called Shady Lady and the Queens features former Steppenwolf member Nick St. Nicholas. In like manner the Dolls, a New York City rock band, sport members such as Johnny Thunder on guitar, who wears red leather cowboy chaps with fringes. Lead singer David Johansen wears skintight trousers and platform heels, while bass guitarist Arthur Kane wears pink tights. Even Mick Jagger now comes out on stage with mascara to further flaunt his often suggested and well known bisexual ambiguities.

Among the best known of today's gay rock entertainers are Lou Reed and David Bowie. Reed, a former member of the Velvet Underground (a rock act produced by the self-proclaimed homosexual Andy Warhol) sings of bleak visions of a nightmare world dominated by drugs. He has become one of the foremost gay rock entertainers with albums like *Transformer*. He is pictured on the jacket in high heels, panty hose, rouge, and mascara. Some of the songs are "Make-up" (a tune about putting on make-up and coming "out of the closets onto the streets") and "Good-night Ladies," which is about the lonely Saturday nights that a perfumed homosexual spends. In another song entitled "Vicious" he sings, "You want me to hit you with a stick when I watch you come / Baby I just want to run away / Why don't you swallow razor blades? / Do you think I am some kind of gay blade?"

David Bowie, who records for RCA Victor, is a British singer-composer-guitarist who boasts in interviews and songs that he is bisexual. His wife is an admitted lesbian, and out of their union have come two children. Wearing orange-hued hair and laced high-heeled boots, he moves in female fashion to a rock beat. He often pretends acts of copulation on stage with other males while singing songs about homosexuals such as "Queen Bitch" and the bisexual experience in "The Width of a Circle." In spite of such perverted extravagance, RCA Victor predicts that he will be the major superstar of this era, and his concerts are sellouts wherever he goes. But the wealth and fame his perversion has brought seems to have only resulted in depression. Recently he announced he was retiring from live performances, even canceling an upcoming American tour reputed to be worth $1.25 million. One rock magazine reported that Bowie expressed the desire to have a tragic death before he hits thirty—that this would be the perfect ending to his career.

All the gay rock groups have to go a long way to beat Alice Cooper. Alice, the male lead singer, claims to be the reincarnation of a seventeenth-century witch and comes out on stage dressed in mascara and women's clothing. A detailed description of this rock group is given in my book *The Day Music Died,* pages 52-55. An Alice Cooper performance is a wedding of perversion and dramatized violence as Alice chops a lifelike doll to pieces, makes love to a writhing snake, and eventually hangs himself on a gallows. In spite of all this, Alice has been asked to lecture at the Eastman School of Music in Rochester, New York. His subject is the art of writing popular music. Cooper now flaunts the commercial success of his ventures by wearing a jacket ornamented with nine stuffed white rats bearing little red sequins where their eyes used to be. The rats are real, and the jacket costs $550. Recently a man charged the stage and tried to kill Alice during a concert. He managed to hit Cooper over the head with a beer bottle. On another occasion an M-80 bomb exploded after being thrown onstage. (Once the drummer found blood flowing down his back, only to discover he had been stabbed by darts hurled from the audience.) Alice knows that some madman could kill him at any time and says, "I really hate the idea of death; it's the only one thing I fear. Just like everyone else I know nothing about it." Alice, whose father is a Baptist minister in Arizona, now owns a forty-room mansion in Greenwich, Connecticut, which sports swastika flags on the ceiling as well as a man-sized doll hanging by the neck in the ballroom.

In mid-1973 Alice had the top chart album, "Billion Dollar Babies," which had already earned over a million dollars on advance sales before it hit the stands. Included is the song, "I Love the Dead," an anthem of necrophilia which Alice sings while having sex onstage with a life-like looking mannequin. A twelve-week tour grossed nearly $6 million and included $150,000 worth of props and a private jet. In mockery his concerts conclude with the playing of a tape recording of Kate Smith singing "God Bless Ameri-

82

ca" while the entire band salutes the flag. Cooper's album *Muscle of Love* (with obvious phallic reference) was planned to include a painting of the group seated at a Thanksgiving dinner in a whorehouse. Alice freely admits, "The whole idea is exploiting sexual perversion. I love to go on stage and torture audiences."

The question must ultimately be raised, "What is a homosexual?" In simple terms that we all could agree upon, homosexuality denotes sexual involvement between members of the same sex. The term *homosexual* can mean either male or female, but it is most commonly applied to describe sexual involvement of one male with another. The term *lesbianism* is commonly used to describe sexual involvement of one female with another. The Christian and non-Christian can all agree on the definition of a homosexual. Disagreement arises from defining what causes a person to prefer homosexuality to heterosexuality.

There does seem to be a basic concensus that homosexuals are not born that way. Most psychiatrists dismiss genetic factors. The existence of identical twins who are divergent in their sexual preferences plays down the genetic argument. There is no valid evidence to support either a physiological, hormonal, or other organic base for homosexuality. From the standpoint of the secular psychological view the cause can invariably be traced to the home and family relationship between parent and child. Homosexuality, especially the male variety, springs forth when there is an abnormal identification with a parent of the same sex. This can be created when the male image is one of an emotionally weak, unaffectionate, and remote father. At the same time the mother is probably dominating, overly intimate, protective, and possessive. The unconcerned father may cause the child to gravitate to the mother, who favors him and encourages a close relationship, even to the point of discouraging any heterosexual interests the child may have. In the case of lesbianism, the same general pattern follows through in reverse. The mother creates a feeling of insecurity in the daughter, causing the child to doubt her feminine identity and attractiveness. Beyond the parent-child relationship, there are other factors that may influence one toward homosexuality.

For some, an adolescent seduction by an older homosexual adult can tip the balances in the life of a disturbed child. An unsatisfactory sex experience, wrong training and knowledge of the biological factors of sex, and a desire to exhibit rebellious or antisocial behavior may be behind the homosexual influence. At the same time, social factors enter into the picture. These may include the enforced isolation of prison or the armed services as well as the immoral environment of a given culture. Certainly the openness, and sometimes favor, with which homosexuality is viewed today is a great factor in influencing youthful curiosity regarding homosexual acts.

It should be noted, however, that anyone may have one or more of these family or environmental influences and still not develop obvious or dormant homosexual tendencies. The child with a home life such as that just described need not fear that he is invariably inclined toward homosexuality. Divorce, the death of one parent, or the personality combination of an agressive father and possessive mother does not necessarily mean that homosexuality is the end result. At the same time, it is just as wrong to assume that a person who has had a sexual experience with an individual of the same sex should be labeled homosexual. One unfortunate experience, sometimes forced upon such an individual, does not constitute homosexuality. Studies have shown that a high percentage of males have engaged in a homosexual act at one time or another; yet a much smaller percentage of that group ever actually becomes deviantly homosexual. Such a person being transplanted to a different family sphere of influence, maturing in years, or developing heterosexual love interests will most probably have little or no residual effects from his homosexual involvement. Some have even had homosexual experiences in high school or college and have completely erased the memory of the act and lived happily adjusted, married lives. If the person having engaged in a homosexual experience begins to fill his mind with pornography or personal experimentation, he may become permanently hooked. The main point to remember is that homosexuality is not chemically caused. Furthermore, even though environment, family, and culture may have been partially influential, the deviant must ultimately make a conscious decision to prefer homosexual relationships. This is a spiritual decision. In reality, no one *is* a homosexual. Homosexuality is not a state of being but rather a noun describing an action of erotic attraction to one of the same sex and culminating in biblically forbidden sexual practices.

Psychologists and sociologists devoid of spiritual principles gauge the effect of homosexuality only in terms of its detrimental influence on society. Some even argue that because it now occurs so frequently and openly that no one can any longer label it as sinful or deviant. Says anthropologist Robin Fox, "What I would define as a sick person in sexual terms would be someone who could not go through the full sequence of sexual activity. I don't think it matters whether the person is of the same sex or not." If however, one takes the Bible seriously, any form of homosexuality cannot be a viable sexual outlet for the Christian. The Bible warns against it and condemns it in harsh language. In fact, the Old Testament prescribed the death penalty for such acts. The law of God not only condemns homosexuality but also views it as a violation of nature itself. It is the Christian view of homosexuality that tells us most about what constitutes this sin.

The Bible in Romans chapter one clearly describes the root of homosexuality. Homosexuality is more than a sexual condition. It is a spiritual condition created when an individual turns his back upon God to pursue sins of the flesh. When the Apostle Paul in I Corinthians 6:9 condemned homosexuals by using the term "effeminate," he was not suggesting that you have to be built like a football player to be a normal male. What we look like may very well be a genetic accident. It is not that one is fragile or delicate in make-up that inclines him toward homosexuality. At the same time it is possible to have genuinely affectionate feelings and a love relationship with someone of the same sex without demeaning that relationship to homosexuality. The warm friendship between David and Jonathan in the Bible was not sexual and stands as a testimony to the wealth and value of brotherly love. Even one with homosexual tendencies need not fear that he is "reprobate" or that God has "given him up." The spiritual key in viewing perversion is found in Romans 1:32 where the Apostle Paul indicates that, those God has "given up" are homosexuals that "not only do the same but have pleasure in them that do them."

Homosexuals can change; the urge can be overcome and need not have a permanent affect upon one's sexuality. For the homosexual who detests his life and desires to be free from its unnatural lust there is hope through the power of the gospel. The sodomite is a sinner just like the rest of the world, and there is salvation in Christ for him. But when a man no longer hates his sins and instead rationalizes and even flaunts it in the face of the church, we must say that he has become reprobate and incurable. For those who despise their homosexual act there is hope, but for the majority who express no desire to change, they have gone beyond the point of no return and nothing but the judgment of God awaits them.

Perhaps the saddest contention made by the homosexual is that his life is truly liberated and "gay." Homosexuals are not gay and they are not happy. The majority are lonely and filled with shame and guilt. They are mentally tortured by feelings of sexual inadequacy and unfulfilled hopes. Even the homosexual who has seared his conscience will still experience great periods of depression. They are not liberated but bound by their unnatural lust; not gay but rather, as Paul said, filled with "covetousness, maliciousness, deceit, and murder."

The homosexual feels persecuted by society as a whole but attacks the church and psychiatric establishment with special zeal. Homosexuals feel that psychiatrists are perhaps most responsible for keeping them from obtaining accepted status in society. Open homosexuality is still grounds for dismissal in most federal agencies, and many employers are reluctant to hire homosexuals. This attitude, the homosexual says, springs from the fact that psychiatrists have labeled the homosexual as sick or mentally disordered. Consequently, militant homosexual groups have vented their rage at various medical groups, including the annual meeting of the American Psychiatric Association in Washington. The group's leader took the stand to declare, "We demand that psychiatrists treat us as human beings, not as patients to be cured." (*Newsweek,* August 23, 1971, page 39) At the 1973 convention in Honolulu the Gay Activists Alliance charged that, "the illness theory of homosexuality is a pack of lies, concocted out of the myths of a patriarchal society for political purposes." The psychiatrists agreed that homosexuality between consenting adults should no longer be regarded as criminal behavior and that it would be dropped from the list of mental aberrations.

To counteract the psychological definition that a homosexual is deviant, art and the mass media have been effective too in proclaiming gay liberation. Homosexuality is now blatantly presented in books, films, and plays. The not-so subtle message is that homosexuality is not only normal but positive and good. Worse yet, much current literature as well as many stage productions emphasize the negative aspects of the male-female relationship and actually discourage a positive attitude toward heterosexuality, portraying the homosexual relationship as preferable and desirable. Films such as *Midnight Cowboy* have made an antihero out of the homosexual. Other gay liberationists such as Kate Millett glorify lesbianism, as in the Millett-produced documentary called *Three Lives.*

In addition to such tactics to help improve their public image, homosexuals have begun to establish the beginning of a distinctly public homosexual life-style complete with organizational structure. Today there are well over a hundred homosexual organizations in existence. They include social clubs and gay bars, as well as counseling centers and communes. Homophile Leagues have been established on dozens of college campuses, and several hundred newspapers, magazines, and newsletters now provide news and internal communication for the gay community. The purpose of all this is to encourage the homosexual to overcome his feelings of inferiority and take pride in his perverted sexual identity. This new psychological self-image is then reinforced by the public admission of homosexuality designed to help the homosexual accept himself as a good and normal person.

The major vent of the homosexual's anger is

against the Church. As a form of counterattack, homosexual clergymen have set up their own churches where they perform all normal religious rites, including marriage. The most notable of these is the well-publicized Metropolitan Community Church of Los Angeles. The Rev. Troy Perry, a former Pentecostal minister from Florida who was expelled for his homosexuality, proclaims the message, "God loves gays, too." *Time* magazine described a worship service in this church of sodomy: "The front rows are filled with a red-robed choir of men and women, hymnals are distributed, an organ plays . . . prayers are read. From a chair at the side, a husky 30-year-old man in vestments abruptly rises, steps swiftly out in front of the makeshift altar and flashing a beguiling smile booms out, ' If you love the Lord this morning, say "Amen." ' "

At least one denomination has arisen, the American Orthodox Church, that maintains ties with Perry's group. Several liberal "straight" churches in San Francisco have offered a haven to homosexuals since the mid-sixties. Glide Memorial Methodist Church sanctions "pledges of commitment between homosexuals." Although Texas Methodists kicked out a minister, Gene Leggett, who proclaimed his homosexuality, the United Church of Christ has at least one openly practicing homosexual minister, Tom Mauer, and has ordained another seminarian. Even the quarterly review of Union Theological Seminary proclaimed that it was "doubtful" that the Bible condemned homosexuality. *Trends,* the United Presbyterian journal, has editorially proposed that the church ordain gay ministers and bless "permanent and faithful" gay unions. The Episcopal Diocese of Michigan has recommended that the denomination admit homosexuals to the ministry and allow church buildings to be used by such groups.

The evangelical church must accept some guilt for its prejudicial attitude toward homosexuals. While one need not soften the scriptural view regarding this depraved sin, it is a terrible prejudice to slander such individuals and classify their sins as worse than adultery or fornication. I myself have felt convicted about using terms such as "fag" and "queer." It is too often been the case that the Church has been unmerciful in its reaction to write off homosexuals as hopeless perverts who deserve only the severest of God's wrath. As with any sinner, the Church must love the homosexual until he has proven himself unrepentant and undesirous of ever turning from his ways, finding only pleasure in them. It is entirely possible that the aforementioned home and family experiences may have created homosexual tendencies within the life of a Christian. He thus has a grave responsibility to keep the commandments of God and abstain from any homosexual conduct. How tragic it is, however, when such a person finds only rejection from the Christian friends he most needs to support him in his efforts to remain obedient to God. I am not suggesting a tolerant compassion that permits deviance but an attitude of love and understanding that prays for the salvation of the homosexual the same as it prays for the salvation of any other sinner whose life has been bound by lust and sins of the flesh.

That the Church could remain silent or tolerant in the view of increased homosexual activity is amazing. The Bible deals explicitly on numerous occasions with this horrible sin. The most lengthy account is found in Genesis 19:1-11. Preceding the destruction of Sodom and Gomorrah, God sent two angels to warn Lot and his family of the impending destruction. Unlike his crude neighbors, Lot was hospitable and generous to these strangers, inviting them to his home and the best accommodations he had. Though they offered to sleep in the open air of the streets, Lot insisted that they abide the night with him.

Upon entering his house, Lot prepared a great feast for them, complete with freshly baked unleavened bread. At the conclusion of the meal the young and old men of Sodom surrounded the house of Lot demanding that the strangers be brought out to them to be sodomized. Shutting the door behind him, Lot stepped outside to beg the men not to homosexually rape the strangers inside. Lot even went beyond the boundaries of hospitality to offer the prostitution of his two virgin daughters to placate the men of Sodom. The Sodomites became even angrier and were so reprobate they preferred the men to Lot's daughters. They threatened to commit sodomy with Lot if he would not let them have the angels inside. Just as they lunged at Lot the men inside reached out and pulled him in, bolting the door. Immediately the angels blinded the Sodomites on the outside. Even then, these men were so wicked that they continued seeking to break the door down until they tired themselves. Not even God's judgment in blinding them changed their corrupt nature and purposes, because their minds as well as their eyes had been blinded by their sinful depravity.

The next day God's judgment was complete as fire and brimstone rained down upon the corrupt cities of Sodom and Gomorrah. I have stood at the side of the Dead Sea and gazed upon that putrid body of water that lies where once Sodom stood. Thirty miles long and ten miles broad, the Dead Sea is just that: *dead.* No living creature is within it. The destruction of Sodom was final and irreparable. The entire valley was laid waste and covered with this salt sea so full of mineral content that an offensive smell rises from it.

To this day, Sodom and Gomorrah and the sins that brought about the destruction of these cities stand throughout Scripture as testimony to God's view of such sinful depravity. The epistle of Jude, verses six and seven, tell us plainly that their destruction is set forth as an example of the judgment of hell. Christ himself validated this example in Matthew 11:23. He warned Capernaum by declaring that if the miracles they saw had been done among the Sodomites, as bad as they were, they would have repented. He ends by declaring that on the day of judgment Sodom would be better off than Capernaum. The message to the homosexual living under today's dispensation of grace is plain. If Sodom, which had no gospel ministry except backslidden Lot, and no Cross to look back to, did not escape the judgment of God, how much more severe will God's penalty be for those who have the full light of Scripture declaring God's displeasure with homosexuality? In a similar manner, Christ declared in Luke 17:28-30 that the sin of Sodom and Gomorrah would be characteristic of the final days before His return. Though our hearts may grieve in seeing the growing numbers and openness of homosexuals, we may at the same time rejoice in knowing that this is a clear indication that the time is soon when "the Son of Man will be revealed."

In 2 Peter 2:9-12, we have a passage of Scripture that again refers to homosexuality. The word in verse ten, *uncleanness,* is the same word used in Romans 1:24. Since Romans 1:21-28 is written explicitly with reference to homosexuality, we can be certain of the meaning of this word in 2 Peter 2:10. The word *uncleanness* is a biblical term for homosexuality and other perversions. It comes from the Greek word *akatharsia* which may be defined as that which is the opposite of purity, such as sodomy, homosexuality, lesbianism, pederasty, and bestiality. *Uncleanness* is also listed in Galatians 5:19 as one of the "works of the flesh." Paul declared in the first letter to the Thessalonians, chapter four, verse seven, "For God has not called us unto uncleanness but unto holiness."

A companion sin to homosexuality is found in a startling development made possible through the surgical advances of modern medical science. Since it was originally disclosed six years ago that American doctors had been performing sex-change operations, five hundred such persons have actually undergone surgical sex change. Unlike the transvestite who still thinks of himself as belonging to the sex into which he was born, the transsexual repudiates his or her biological sex and often literally tries to pass as a member of the opposite sex. Doctors who have tried to make the mind match the body have now decided to make the patient's body match his mind.

The surgery, most commonly performed on male transsexuals wanting to change to female, involves removal of the genitals and construction of an artificial vagina and in some cases breast enlargement. In the case of a female transsexual, the breasts are removed, a hysterectomy is performed, and a penis is actually constructed. In addition, the hormones that stimulate secondary sex characteristics are adapted accordingly. Such operations costing more than $10,000 have been performed by Johns Hopkins University and at nearly a dozen American medical centers.

One medical center at the University of Minnesota did two dozen such operations under a research program financed entirely at the expense of the state taxpayers. From a medical standpoint the sex-reassigned transsexuals appear to develop into normal heterosexuals. Some of the patients have capitalized upon their unusual condition for publicity, but most have been anxious to keep their lives private. No one knows how many transsexuals are in this country, but it is certain that more are going to be seeking such operations as the publicity and proficiency of them grows.

Why is God against sexual change or perversion? My answer is one I am sure you have not read before, for I do not know that anyone else has treated the subject of homosexuality in this perspective. I believe that homosexuality today is a direct result of the influence that Darwinian evolution has had upon the philosophic thought of modern man. If, as evolution teaches, life grows spontaneously out of gases formed into complex organic compounds, including sugars, purines, and amino acids, then such a primordial "soup" was nonsexual in its origin. Any highschool biology student can testify that evolution teaches that sexual characteristics are acquired through the evolving complexities of high life forms. A study of protozoan biological evolution shows that at one time in his history, man by the standards of evolution was at least asexual and possibly bisexual as well. Upon this premise, man was not specifically created as a sexually defined being but rather has acquired his sexual characteristics only as a result of the evolutionary process designed to propagate his life form in the most expedient means possible. With this in mind, God's absolutes of conduct are cast aside in favor of sociological morality. Therefore, to accept the biblical rejection of homosexuality, one must first ask the question, "What is man?"

From the biblical standpoint man had an absolute beginning as a moral creature created out of nothing by the word of God. Made in the image of God, Adam was a living thing with conscious life. How ridiculous to assume that the ordered creation of man could have arisen spontaneously from disorder. Can unthinking atoms create intelligent thought? Nowhere is this observed in nature, in spite of the catch phrases used by the evolutionists, such as "random mutation and natural selection." The law of biogenesis teaches that life comes from life, and man's life came from the life in the breath of God." If this, then, is our basis for acknowledging the origin of man, then we clearly understand why God is against homosexuality.

The record of Genesis declares in chapter one, verse twenty-seven, "So God created man in his own image, male and female created he them." Like the creation of Adam, the creation of Eve was a special, distinct act of God with an absolute beginning. Thus we see that our sexual characteristics are God-defined and had a God-determined beginning. Even those evolutionists who would like to trace our ancestory to those ape-like creatures on earth today would be hard pressed to justify homosexuality in that life form. In the book *The Shadow of Man,* Jane Goddall describes her experiences of living among chimpanzees in the African rain forest of Tanzania. Although affection among those of the same sex was observed, she concluded, "Never have we seen anything that could be regarded as homosexuality in chimpanzees." Not even our supposed predecessors violate God's law of sexual distinction. Is it any wonder that in 2 Peter 2:12 the apostle speaks of homosexuals as "brute beasts" no better than animals? Homosexuality is wrong because it defies the Genesis account of man's origin by ignoring the God-ordained sexual distinctiveness built into man and woman through the creative power of God. Worse yet, it mocks the love of Christ for His Church, which throughout Scripture is portrayed in terms commensurate with the sexual relationship between man and woman.

What is the effect of today's gay liberation? Sadly, it seems that more homosexuals are accepting their state as normalcy and feeling less guilty about it. While they proclaim that "gay is good," even their most eloquent spokesmen sometimes raise nagging doubts. Merle Miller, a prominent writer and proclaimed homosexual, wrote, "I suppose if I had been given a choice I would prefer to have been straight." Much simplistic rhetoric is telling homosexuals that their way of sexual behavior is equal in value to heterosexuality. If such irresponsible conclusions persist and an image of homosexual "normality" is propagated, there will be more homosexually inclined people who will follow their urge without hesitation. Worse yet, those who live such perverted lives might encourage those with latent homosexual tendencies to feel less guilty about it. Thus, some adolescents, instead of seeking heterosexuality to resolve their confusion, will accept the immediate gratification of homosexuality because spokesmen have told them that they are normal and healthy.

There is already evidence that the impact of open homosexuality has deeply influenced the unconscious thinking of Americans regarding sexual determination. A New York psychologist just found that young people are undergoing a psychological reversal in sexual identity that matches their changing fashion styles as well as the changing attitude toward homosexuality. His conclusions are based on responses to the famous Rorschach ink-blot test. The images in the test are supposed to give insight into personality structure. The way in which a person responds to a particular image shows his sexual identity. According to a report issued in the *Journal of Psychology*, ink-blot tests conducted in the 1950s showed that an image which fifty-one percent of the males responded to as being male now only gets a sixteen percent response. In fact, fifty-one percent of the males today now see the image as being female. Dr. Fred Brown, who conducted the study, traces this reverse in sexual identity to the belittling of fathers and mothers on television. He observed, "Patients do recover, and another study ten years from now may show a different picture. On the other hand, patients and societies also die." Perhaps the ultimate expression of homosexual despair was that of a reputed avant-garde artist who amputated his own genitals inch by inch and had the event recorded on photographs as he bled to death.

In spite of the utter depravity and the binding power of this sin, there is hope for the homosexual.

Let me share with you a testimony of one of the most dramatic deliverances from homosexuality that I have ever witnessed. I will change the names of the individuals involved and simply make reference to the homosexual who experienced deliverance through exorcism as John Doe.

Mr. Doe came to me for counseling during one of my recent crusades. He spoke to me after a service in which I had dealt with demonism and the occult. For some years Mr. Doe had been plagued with homosexuality. Significantly, John wanted to be free from this enslaving lust. He had no desire whatsoever to remain homosexual and with tearful regret told of the times that "out of nowhere" the homosexual drive would come upon him.

After extensive counseling I concluded that, first of all, Mr. Doe genuinely desired to be freed.

He did not excuse his homosexuality nor did he "find pleasure in it." I also noted that his description of the times the urge for homosexual relationships would strike him was quite singular. It seemed that for little-understood reasons he would become possessed with a homosexual desire and immediately crave the body of another man. With the strength of several men he would rape or assault whoever might be near him. After such episodes he was filled with pangs of guilt and regret, not being able to understand why he had acted in such a depraved manner. He also commented that at such times severe anger and violence would grip him. The conclusion seemed inevitable: demonism was definitely an influencing factor.

I shall never forget the morning that John came to the end of his rope and desperately cried out for the delivering power of God's Spirit. One must be cautious in diagnosing any psychic disorder as originating in demonism. If such a diagnosis is wrong, irreparable damage can be done. On the other hand, if demonism is genuinely discerned through the perceptive spirit of the counselor, he should not be hesitant to force Satan's hand and demand that he release his victim. Through counseling, John became aware that his problem was due to a spiritual force beyond him, one to which he had become enslaved through previous involvement in pornography and X-rated movies.

I asked John to be seated on a couch opposite the chair in which I was seated facing him. Without touching him or going near him, I exercised the power and authority in the name of Jesus and commanded the unclean demon to come forth. For some time John wept and shook uncontrollably as if in a fit of nervous depression. I asked him to pray with me and, fortunately, the demon's hold on his life was not to the extent of totally possessing his will. John himself cried forth for deliverance from God. Finally, the power of the unclean spirit was broken, and I spoke with God-endued authority, "You vile demon of lust and homosexuality, release your hold on John's life."

At that moment John was thrown off the couch by the demon, flew into the air, and struck the ground with a thud. He writhed about, grabbing his throat as if some unseen force (indeed there was) were trying to choke him. He gagged, vomited, and finally collapsed in a sweating, exhausted heap. There was no doubt about it. John was free!

The next few days and months were difficult ones for Mr. Doe. He was in touch with me by letter and by telephone. On one occasion he did lapse by visiting an X-rated movie. This oppressive spirit came upon him and it was only as a result of a long-distance phone call in which he contacted me that the spirit was kept from reentering his life. John immediately began to actively engage himself in a local church body where he found the fellowship of Christian friends. This active Christian life helped to build his strength, and it was with a great source of joy and satisfaction that I received a letter recently from John. He spoke of his forthcoming marriage and wrote:

> I met Joan about three years ago. She and I have been together very often. We were very close

101

friends, because I was not capable of loving a woman. If I know what real love is, I do love her now more than I have ever loved anyone. She is a great Christian girl with a faith in God that is unshakable. She knows and has seen what God has done to my life. She joined my church last week and we plan to work together for the Lord. Bob, I am very happy, and I am sure that God is in this. I want to thank you for letting God use you to help me find *real* life in Christ. I appreciate you very much and extend Christian love to you and your lovely wife. May God bless your ministry.

There is hope for the homosexual in the power of Jesus Christ, for the Bible declares in Romans 5:20, "Where sin abounded, grace did much more abound." Homosexuals are not distinguished by God for special condemnation. The fire and brimstone poured out on Sodom and Gomorrah was not only for their homosexuality but all manner of evil. In a similar vein, the first chapter of Romans is not directed toward homosexuals alone. Before the condemnation of that chapter the Apostle Paul states in verse eighteen, "The wrath of God is against all ungodliness." In writing to the church at Corinth the Apostle Paul indicated that some members of that congregation had been homosexuals in times past but now were followers of Christ.

Let us remember that it is not the sin of homosexuality that damns the soul of a man any more than the sin of adultery or fornication. These and other sins are but the expression of a life alienated from God. It is sin that consigns the soul to everlasting punishment: the sin of rejecting Christ as Lord and Savior. All who have not been cleansed by the blood of Christ stand in equal condemnation before the throne of God. If there is hope for the homosexual, salvation from the sin of Sodom, then thank God that there is most assuredly hope for any sinner who will come in repentance to Jesus Christ.

5

Rakashan

Ours is an age that declared, "God is dead," and loosed this generation upon an existential sea. But God has created a spiritual hunger in man that must be satisfied. For many, the occult has been more than a quest of curiosity, and Satanism and witchcraft have filled the gap for those who are victims of modern man's spiritual bankruptcy. The press periodically reports the horrors of such consequences.

There is another side to the story. Thousands of youth are turning to Christ, including some who have been deeply involved in the occult. All across America I find young people formerly bound by demonic enslavement now set free through the power of the gospel. Their stories are an encouraging note in this Aquarian age.

104

Out of the many testimonies of such deliverance that I have encountered, one stands out in my mind as being perhaps the most dramatic evidence of progressive occult enslavement and subsequent liberation. The first time I met Pete was during a crusade in his home city. Earlier in the week I had issued an appeal common in many of my campaigns. Imploring the young people to take a separated stand for Christ, I asked them to bring for destruction the hard-rock albums that had previously hindered their Christian lives. Among the other people standing at the altar, Pete looked no different—just another teenager desiring to make a full commitment of his life to Jesus Christ. After prayer, each teen-ager methodically broke his records as a public testimony to the inner work of the Holy Spirit, breaking the chains of sin on his life. Watching the other young people take this stand for Christ, Pete realized that this was an area he had not yet surrendered to the Lord. Consequently, the next night he returned and destroyed $550 worth of his own albums.

At the time I had no idea what a dramatic step this was. Thousands of youth come in my crusades to make similar stands for Christ. But as I talked further with Pete, I was soon to learn that his story was much different from the average. In subsequent counseling sessions he shared with me his story regarding the depths of evil to which he had gone in searching for spiritual reality. In this chapter, I share with you his story, the testimony on one who innocently became entrapped in Satan's clutches and was nearly destroyed as the result.

Pete's occult curiosity began early in life. He can still recall as a child being interested in ghosts and formulating ideas regarding their existence. The other side of the spiritual realm was first encountered when Pete accompanied his parents on a summer vacation to a southern city infamous for its occult history. There, while visiting a haunted house, he saw his first ghost. He had heard no tales or stories regarding ghost activities, but as they toured the building he realized there were mysterious things that he knew about it. He remarked to the tour guide what his observations were. She agreed that what he said was true and was amazed as to how he could have known such things. This started Pete thinking about what his beliefs were in relationship to the world about him and what he might discover regarding the hereafter. He wondered if he had a right to even know about such things.

After the ghost encounter, Pete discovered that dreams were starting to come true, and he wondered if perhaps he might have some God-given ability to understand the unknown. Even though he had been raised in a religious home and was subsequently confirmed at the age of twelve, he knew nothing at all about the Word of God. Consequently, he made no search in the Scriptures to answer his questions. Even his pastor was of no help.

As he grew into adolescence Pete realized that something was drawing him, pulling his thinking. He felt that he knew things other people did not know. There was no question in his mind that he had an understanding of the supernatural. He sensed presences and at times would see things

106

others did not. Was he losing his mind? This was the question he often asked but was confident of his sanity. When he tried to talk about spirits, some were interested but most shunned him.

During junior high Pete discovered that he was not progressing emotionally on a par with his peers, and others considered him weird because of his occult curiosity. As a result he became somewhat of a loner, and in high school Pete's emotional difficulties increased. He was intellectually equal to his peers but had an understanding of life and the world around that caused others to ostracize him. All the while his interest in the supernatural grew.

It was at this time that the era of Flower Power was ushered in to America's life-styles. Not only were the hippies gaining prominence with their countercultural idiosyncrasies, but also (as I have traced in my book *Hippies, Hindus and Rock and Roll)* Eastern religions were gaining popular acceptance. Then one day Pete was handed a book entitled *Yoga for Christians.* It was supposed to be a book of just exercises. Soon Pete discovered that yoga is comprised of more than just calisthenic maneuvers. (The precepts of yoga come from Hindu theology and often include, even in the early stages, the recitation of mantras, taken from the sacred Hindu texts.) He found that it is impossible to take part in any religion, no matter how small that part may be, without being eventually given over to it. For Pete, yoga evolved into a belief about not only the human body but also a worship of the mind and self-esteem in the power of one's will. Finally its ultimate purpose unfolded: the building up of the mind to accomplish some supernatural task. At the same time the pantheistic aspects of yoga took hold of Pete and he found himself worshiping and relating with nature. He would sit in the park watching birds and trees, seeking to communicate with the god of the universal spirit that he believed to be in them.

As his involvement in yoga increased Pete found himself experimenting with mind techniques and mental projections. He gradually developed what he thought were his own personal philosophies about the unknown in the world around him. At first, it was all a game, but gradually Pete found that the people who once thought he was weird now listened to his ideas with interest. As an aid in this search he began to watch every television program that dealt with the occult. He read books such as *The Exorcist,* fascinated by those who had dedicated their lives to discovering psychic phenomena.

Pete was not content to keep his findings to himself. In school he issued reports on ghosts, UFOs, and the reading of auras. At this point it might be well to explain to the reader what an aura is. About each person is an atmosphere of an emanation of colors, similar to the pattern in a rainbow. Mediumistic spiritualists have the ability to see these hues which are invisible to the naked eye. By reading these colors and corresponding them to a chart of characteristics, a medium may discern a person's physical, spiritual, and emotional nature. I cannot explain how it works or what creates the aura of each person, but I know that its existence is real.

On one occasion I attended a university lecture

of a medium. At the conclusion a student asked him to read the auras of those who were present. Even though I was seated somewhat obscurely at the rear of the classroom, the medium chose me as an example. According to the medium, the aura about my body indicated that at one time I had made a definite choice to abandon a previously decided-upon profession in life (at one time I had planned to go into medicine and in fact pursued premedical training at a university). Now, the medium told me, I was pursuing my life's work and was interested in above all following the teachings of Jesus. He told the other students that I was an extremely spiritually inclined person.

From a friend, Pete learned the occult art of reading auras. He felt as though he had already been given this gift and only needed to be aware that he possessed such ability. Even after his conversion to Christ, Pete could still read auras. Though he knew it was wrong, at times he found himself resorting to this occult practice. It was particularly useful at church. There he would seek to discern the spiritual character of his fellow Christians. This developed a judgmental spirit that made him so critical it hindered his relationship to others in the Body of Christ. Finally, after much prayer, he asked the Lord to take away the ability to read auras.

As a result of his development of psychic powers, Pete became an object of interest, and his classmates came to him with questions. From this Pete saw that young people of his age were searching spiritually for something that could change their lives. Everyone wanted to be something different than he was. So sought after was Pete for spiritual guidance that he began to take the "fun and games" as a serious occupation. He decided that it was time to directly consort with spiritual powers.

It was not long afterwards that he held his first seance as the result of information he had obtained from watching one on television. So good did he become that the somewhat elderly ladies from a local church missionary society invited him to conduct a seance at their monthly meeting. He did so, much to their glee and interest.

Pete's bedroom in his home became the focal point for spirit consultations. During the day his room was arranged into a den for occult activities. A major tool in his seances was the Ouija board because so many people knew about it and it was quick to capture their interest. He found that most anyone could get a Ouija board to work if they would submit themselves to it. The results were surprisingly accurate.

At first the seances were simple. All he sought was some kind of sign, the moving of the counter on the Ouija board or a sound that was unexplainable. But the more people responded to the seances, the more spectacular signs of confirmation were sought. Some asked to see images. The first such request was granted when Pete deliberately rigged things to produce a reflection. But subsequent seances needed no such naturalistic help. When Pete asked for a sign, a candle flame rose higher and higher for fifteen minutes. With phosphorescent chalk he drew a circle, and everyone was asked to concentrate his thoughts on it. Each saw a large ball of light appear. Pete looked and saw a cylinder rising to the ceiling.

Next, he had a vision of a person who doubled over in pain and died. The stage of pure experimentation had passed.

Satan was taking Pete step by step, deeper and deeper. A friend of his parents gave him the book *God's World,* the catechism of spiritualism. The volume recounts more than sixty seances in which conversations with spirits supposedly revealed the truth regarding the world about us. *God's World* taught Pete how to make contact with spirits and what to do after it was made. Pete also read other books but was determined to develop his own theories. By this time, others had gathered about him, and they too wanted to do things a little bit different for their own unique search. No one in the group, including Pete, was sure where their direction was coming from, but they knew that they were being guided and that they had to do what was revealed to them.

At this time Pete felt directed to go beyond mere seances. He moved to a back bedroom in the house and first covered the windows with a heavy, black canvas. With florescent paint, stars were mapped on the ceiling. Everything was removed from the room in order to furnish and arrange it according to spirit direction. The dresser for clothes was left, but was placed in the closet to be out of the way. Since music was used to create a proper atmosphere, the stereo was put in the closet as well with speakers mounted inside the room. Small pallets were placed about the room on the floor to serve as cushions during the day and as a bed at night. Perhaps most importantly, an altar was erected complete with a small Buddha, flowers, the Ouija board, and incense. When

I questioned Pete as to how he knew in what manner to arrange the room, he answered that somehow at the time it just seemed right to do.

After the room was arranged, sitar music was played on the phonograph. In these Indian raga sounds Pete had found a conducive medium for mind expansion and the invitation of spirits. The album chosen was *Music for Meditation* by Ravi Shankar. He sat down and began to go through yoga positions while asking, "Who has control of the altar?" All the time he kept a tape recorder going to hear later what had taken place. Throughout his meditation the volume on the record player sounded to him and the others present as if it were crescendoing and subsiding in a cyclical fluctuation. Afterwards when he replayed the tape recording its sound was normal and stable throughout. He was now convinced by this supernatural occurence that the room was dedicated to Satan. So real was the demonic presence inside that his mother was frightened and would not go near. Their maid said the room was haunted, and even the household pet dog refused to enter.

With all in order, Pete decided that it was time to engage in mind-traveling and out-of-the-body experiences. The reader may be somewhat skeptical as to whether or not such "soul excursions" are actually possible. Occult studies reveal that some Tibetan spiritualists claim the ability to leave their bodies and travel great distances. Many Western mediums also purport to have engaged in astral projections. On one occasion Pete left his body to visit the home of a friend. All evening he watched the actions of this acquain-

112

tance and the next day at school confronted the fellow, offering to tell him all that he had done the evening before. Imagine the shock of this friend, who had been home the whole evening with no one present in the house, when he heard Pete detail his activities for the night.

Other spiritualistic experiences were enhanced by black light posters that were hung on the wall to help induce hallucinogenic experiences similar to those obtained on LSD. Interestingly enough, no one in the group was allowed to take drugs of any kind. It was felt that this abstinence would give a clearer view of what was happening. Furthermore, no one could accuse them of drug-induced illusions when they told others. This helped to verify their experiences and drew an even larger crowd of sympathetic followers. Drugs might have been used by Satan to extend their involvement, but dope was not needed because of the involvement already given to the spiritualistic directions.

To take the place of drugs, Satan used music. They found that certain types of music had the qualities of being able to take them "up" or "down." Some turned the mind inward while other music forms incited wildness and violence. When yielded to the music, they allowed themselves to be totally open and susceptible to whatever would come their way. Acid rock was the most prevalent music used, but not the only one. They went "up" on rock and usually came "down" on some of the more unstructured forms of classical music. Indian raga music, because of its free-flowing nature, was particularly useful as mentioned earlier.

Incense played an important role as well. I have long been alarmed at the way in which incense is used by Christian young people. When speaking out against this in my crusades, I have invariably been confronted with demands to provide some concrete reasons for objection. I suppose that my reaction is in part due to my overseas experiences at pagan, religious rituals. A visit to any Buddhist or Hindu temple will find the fragrance of incense surrounding these heathen altars. The pagan believes that as the smoke of the incense rises skyward, spirits are petitioned to descend and inhabit the aroma. Perhaps in my own mind when I smell incense I immediately connotate it with the heathen rituals that I have seen and the thousands that I have watched bow before altars pervaded with the scent of incense. Though some would counter that incense was used in the Old Testament, its purposes were entirely different from the pagan utilization. Furthermore, there is no New Testament account of incense burned before an altar under the New Covenant. Believers are to be "a sweetsmelling savour" (Ephesians 5:2) to God by their testimonies.

In addition, I object to the use of incense because Eastern religious thought is so prevalent today. All practitioners of Eastern religions use incense, and a Christian who does so may cause some doubt about his testimony from connotations with its pagan intent. Pete's use of incense certainly supports my apprehensions. As he explains it, incense was burned not only for sweetness of the aroma, but it also brought a warm feeling and a fragrance that induced a spirit-inviting atmosphere.

114

In additon to music and incense an extensive amount of symbolism was employed. By this time Pete was deep into astrology and study of the zodiac, but it was not a typical interest. He developed his own theories of what characteristics should be applied to each house of the zodiac and made his own predictions that were surprisingly accurate. In all of this he became somewhat of an amateur psychologist, telling people what they had done and why. But the more things progressed the more he became convinced that though he was getting answers he was not getting truth, the whole answer. Somehow Pete felt that he was deliberately being confused.

No form of occultism was to be left out. Pete was given as a gift a set of tarot cards, in particular the gypsy-witch version. (Tarot cards are an ancient form of divination whereby through the laying of cards the future is supposedly discerned. Our present deck and system of playing is derived from the tarot, and much of Christianity's opposition to cards stemmed from this original, occult attachment.) The more Pete read cards the better he got. He not only read the past but in the instance of one girl he foretold a death in her family and a subsequent fight before the reading of the will. All was eventually confirmed. Pete felt that he was not reading the cards but actually looking into the person. Next came the tarot deck called "Tarot for the Aquarian Age", given as a present from a follower in his cult. The moment he opened the deck the cards seemed to speak to him. He sensed that this deck was not normal; there was a power behind it. Even other occultists who read cards came to him confessing that his predictions were more accurate than any of theirs had ever been. As Pete now describes it, he did not control the cards but they controlled him, telling him what to do and when to do it.

Even though Pete did not understand entirely what was happening and was at times frightened by the spirits that he felt, he continued on. More and more groups began to meet, and each weekend became a time of greater experimentation. They constantly sought to heighten their sensitivity until they reached the point where they could actually "see" music, "feel" colors, and relate physically to tangible objects about them. Out of all this, the organization of a cult finally formed. The group began meeting regularly for psychic exploration, and a high council was formed with Pete designated as the high priest. Only nineteen years of age, yet here he was the Satanist leader for a sizable cult in one of America's largest cities.

Now it was decided that just feeling the presence of spirits was not enough. They wanted to see them and actually sit down and talk face to face. It was decided that a conjuring would be held.

For some time a friend had been wanting to join the group. Now the cult could accomplish a double purpose by initiating the friend and having him serve as the patsy for the conjuring by being the recipient of the spirit they would petition. When the night arrived Pete began by setting the room in order.

His first act was to set a table in the center. A mirror was placed on the table and a pentagram, (an inverted star of David expressing anti-God sentiment with the upper apexes representing the horns of the supposed goat-head satanic symbol) was drawn in the center. Pete had never read what to do for a conjuring, but something told him that the mirror represented lust and the pentagram Satan. A circle was drawn on the floor, and Pete lit three candles, setting them outside the circumference. That same something told him that the candles represented the trinity of God, and that setting them outside the circle not only acknowledged the existence of God but denied Him access to what would take place inside. The friend was told to sit in the center and place his hands on the table looking into the mirror. Next the cultists joined hands and danced and chanted around the initiate. From a rock album by Vanilla Fudge a song entitled "Season of the Witch" was chosen for the musical liturgy.

Everything was designed to properly approach and petition satanic powers. All that took place was to be unnatural and against God. Since God represents stillness and peace, they became loud, aggressive, and hysterical. They purposed to show no respect for anyone or anything. Around and around they danced, chanting to the initiate, to the room, and to the air around the room, "God of fear, lust, light, and pain, Rakashan, come forth!"

Over and over they chanted until a strange warmth entered the room. It was during the winter months and Pete had deliberately cut the heat off. What they felt was a muggy, deep heat. Suddenly, everyone stopped and looked at the initiate in the circle. His eyes were wildly dilated and his flesh began to crawl up and down his body as if every organ inside were being torn into pieces. Pete looked at the young man before the altar and screamed, "Who are you?"

The eyes of the young man stared back, with a hellish gaze. "Who are you!" Pete cried in desperation.

From within the initiate's body came the reply, "Who did you summon?"

"You know who I called," Pete answered, somewhat terrified. "Tell me, who are you?"

"I am third only to Satan—Rakashan. I have come that you might learn," the voice solemnized.

That was enough. Pete and his friends, were so frightened they wanted nothing whatsoever to do with Rakashan. Though nothing quite as terrifying as this had happened, other spirits had been summoned and sent away, so Pete knew the procedure. Immediately they began to reverse everything they had done, including dancing in the opposite direction. This time they chanted, "Rakashan, god of fear, lust, light, and pain, depart."

They chanted while Pete progressively blew out each candle. Finally when they sensed that Rakashan had gone the young man kneeling in the circle jumped to his feet and ran for the bathroom. He vomited uncontrollably until everything in his stomach was gone; then he vomited blood. The friend had been in a complete trance and didn't know what had happened. He only knew that he was violently ill and his body ached with pain.

Pete sat down and thought upon what had just happened. He now realized that he was not controlling the spirits as he had thought. Satan had been leading him on, letting him think that he was

118

running the show just to get the group together. The promise of power, attention, and friendship had only been the devil's tool to use him as an instrument. Pete had become aware that the show was running him and that Rakashan had not left the room, even though he had left the body of the initiate. Demon spirits do not come unless they are invited and leave only when they are ready, unless another power (which the Bible teaches is Christ) drives them away. During the next two years Rakashan was to torment that room and everyone who entered into it.

Still, Pete did not stop his satanic practices. Fascinated with mind-traveling, the cult engaged in new out-of-the-body experiences, but each time they returned they found their bodies had been used while they were gone. In many instances an unnatural sense of fatigue had set in, and at other times they would awake from a trance to find their bodies entangled. Sometimes physical injury had been inflicted, and they found themselves fighting among each other. To this day Pete has no explanation for what may have happened while they were out of their bodies.

The next Halloween, another conjuring was scheduled. Rather nonchalantly Pete announced at school one day about this upcoming activity. When the night arrived, people from all over the city showed up, including one young girl who had constantly expressed the desire to join their group. She was determined to contact Satan and informed the cult that they would never be able to have any manifestations unless they quit using white magic. A circle was drawn and she stepped into it, telling Pete to stay away. With earnest desperation she cried, "I've come to make a pact with you, Satan."

Four candles had been lit and set about the circle, one in front of her, one behind her, and one on either side. Suddenly winds came up from all four directions and dogs all about the neighborhood began to howl. Each candle was immediately extinguished, except the one directly in front of her. At this point about ten people jumped to their feet indicating they wanted no part of what was going on and immediately left. As a result the events of the evening were terminated.

But something important did happen that night. A boy who had heard about the conjuring from a friend came and showed Pete a book, *The Herbiverac Massonic Rosicrucian Book of Techniques*. As Pete now described it, "This guy just happened to hear about the conjuring, he just happened to come, he just happened to have bought this book at an obscure bookstore, and he just happened to forget the book and leave it at my house for the time it took me to read it. I never saw him again but found in the book a phone number that belonged to a friend of his. The friend came by in a few days to get the book. Later I learned that it was a rare and valuable book and one highly sought after by Satanists. When I look back upon all the information that I got out of it, I have no doubt but that Satan, had it deliberately left there for a reason."

The spirit sessions in Pete's room continued, and all the while he noticed that it was being filled with a heavier atmosphere. One night a member came with a rubber knife. When he displayed it they suddenly all went into a murderous frenzy for over an hour until everyone in the room had been "killed." Looking back, Pete recalls that they loved every minute of it. If the knife had been real Pete believes they would have actually murdered someone!

By this time the seances had degenerated to sex parties. When the lights went out men and women could do whatever they wanted on their own pallet without anyone bothering them. Pete knew that he was simply being used to bring all of this about.

The next turning point in his life came some months later when he awakened at two in the morning. At first he couldn't understand why he should awaken at such an unusual hour with a full day of school ahead of him. Then he realized that the atmosphere of the room was unusually heavy. He glanced at his side and beheld a sight that chilled his blood. It was an exact negative of himself, a thing lying there touching his body. Somehow he was out of his own body and saw this thing trying to move inside of him. He knew intuitively that it brought death with it! Not knowing why, and never having done so before in his life, Pete cried out to God, "Don't allow this to happen. Lord, if there be any mercy in You, deliver me. God save me." He knew that the thing was the embodiment of Rakashan coming to take him. He didn't understand why, but somehow, God had delivered him.

It was yet to be nine months before Pete would come to find the reality of Christ in his life. During this time a boy joined the group who said that he was going to teach them a new way to find truth. After about two weeks the members discovered that this new way would be homosexuality. Later Pete was to learn from other sources that homosexuality eventually comes into every satanic cult. This vile form of perversion is Satan's ultimate attempt to destroy any remaining elements of morality or decency and turn people totally over to the worship of demons. As he now looks back on those days Pete's insights are provocative.

"I know now that homosexuality is not a mental disorder or a disease that can be treated by medical science," Pete explains. "It is a spirit. I knew respectable young men who would never have consented to a thing like that, but the moment that boy touched them they just gave up to him. I was astounded, but they did." The new member had started the homosexuality by suggesting the practice of so-called "sensitivity" yoga in which two or more people touch and engage in sexual exercises. The purpose was to break down all inhibitions. The cult went on to meditate in the nude and commit acts of perversion that left many of them ill the next day.

It was at this stage that Pete realized something had to give. About two months later he was seated in his yard one day carving an idol for a friend of his. The girl for whom the idol was carved had accused him of using magic to make her things disappear. The idol was to serve as an amulet.

A friend came by and told Pete about a musical group that was singing in a nearby park. There had been several political rallies that week, and since Pete was at one time sympathetic with the SDS he had some interest. But at this time he was not at all inclined to hear just another speech. The friend, a member of the cult, said he had heard some good music and suggested that the two of them go together to see what it was all about.

When they arrived at the park, Pete was shocked to hear a church youth choir singing and testifying about their personal faith in Jesus Christ. Amazingly, these young people had something that he had been searching for all this time. He had only gotten more confused, but they *knew* what they were talking about. The friend who invited Pete was not interested in hearing about Christ and wanted to go back home.

But when Pete got there he found something drawing him to the park, and so he got in his car and returned. It had been a cold evening, and yet this group of young people loved that audience enough to stand up there, as uncomfortable as they were, and tell them about their faith. This intrigued Pete. He couldn't imagine them caring for someone else that much.

When the choir was finished, Pete noticed that the director had the same name as a friend he had known some years ago. Out of curiosity he went backstage to meet the director and see if he was related to this friend. The director informed Pete that he was not related to the friend. They talked for a while, and Pete offered to assist the group in moving the musical equipment back to the church.

After arriving at the church they put the piano and other instruments back in place. A few of the young people were standing about conversing with Pete when he began to share with them his beliefs regarding communication with spirits. One of the young men interrupted to tell him that what he was doing was wrong. Pete countered by saying that he had been to ministers and they couldn't help him and couldn't see anything wrong with what he was doing. It was then that one of the teenagers opened a Bible and showed Pete what he had been needing to hear for years, the Scriptures from God forbidding any form of occultism. The Word of God is powerful. For the first time in his life Pete realized that he had been treading on forbidden ground. He dropped his head and cried, "God, help me!"

That night when he went home he found himself asking, "Who are these young people? What do they believe?" He was further intrigued when he awakened the next morning to realize that the nightmares that had been plaguing his mind for three years were gone.

Determined to find out more about what it was these young people had, he returned to their church that next Sunday morning. When the message was concluded and the invitation was given he went forward to the altar, but when he was counseled with and tried to pray he found it impossible to do so. Pete had summoned spirits but he didn't know how to pray to God.

His description of what happened next is exciting. "I reached out to grab the hands of the two men who were praying on either side of me. Something went through my body as if I were grasping hold of an electrical wire. It shocked but I didn't want to let go. That power surged through my body until all the evil was burned out and I was able to ask Jesus Christ to come into my life."

To those who know Pete now there is no question about the reality of his testimony for the Lord. In straightforward language he tells others what Christ now means to him. "That Sunday morning began a new way of living that I had never seen before in all my life. Things haven't been the easiest since then but I now have a satisfaction beyond explanation. In the Christian life there is always something new to find, something else to discover in the joy of reading God's Word. I thank God that he spared me from what I was."

This testimony stands as a living witness to the power of Christ that can liberate men from occult bondage no matter how serious it may be. So great is the transforming grace of His love that Pete now has the call to the ministry upon his life and intends to enter full-time Christian service. The story of his former life is being tragically repeated thousands of times across America, but the testimony of his present life is also being reiterated by young people who have been snatched from the grip of Satan by the power of the Holy Spirit. Pete's body that Rakashan desired is today the temple of God.

6

Incubus

A young, New York housewife finds herself trapped and manipulated by a coven of witches. Eventually, she is forced into the experience of incubus (sexual intercourse with a materialized demon spirit). Out of this union, birth is given to a child which is half-human and half-devil.

A science fiction horror tale? Testimony from a Salem witch trial? The recounting of a grisly, medieval drama? Wrong on all three counts! What I have just described is the plot for a 1968 movie that grossed $40 million and now ranks among the top fifty of all time, *Rosemary's Baby*.

Ask those who have been involved in Satanism or witchcraft what attracted them to such an esoteric group and the answer will be one of two things: the promise of power or the lure of immoral sexual gratification. The latter has a particularly appealing attractiveness to youth in today's permissive society.

The prospect of uninhibited sexual pleasure has often been the bait to involve young people in occult practices. Some who would have been appalled at the prospect of worshiping the devil have become entwined in such practices because unlimited fornication is so often a part of these rituals. Indeed, the second and third degrees of witchcraft of necessity include promiscuous sexual intercourse. The Black Mass itself is conducted over the prostrate body of a nude woman lying on an altar. For the female initiate, witchcraft cults often demand that she give up her virginity by having group sex with the male members.

It seems to me that our age is characterized by an overwhelming curiosity regarding the occult and an illicit craving for sexual experimentation. Incubus is an excellent satanic vehicle for satisfying both. In the Middle Ages the Witches' Sabbats were celebrated by degenerate orgies of indiscriminate lust. Limitless sexual indulgence was achieved by the ultimate act of perversion: the supernatural union of a human and a demon. Strange it is that in our "enlightened" age, human-demonic sexual relations should be having a revival. Unfortunately, this is precisely the case.

Incubus refers to sexual relationships between a human female and a materialized demon that assumes male form. Succubus is sexual intercourse engaged in by a human male and a materialized demon that assumes female proportions. The reader may be tempted to scoff since few realize that invisible, intangible spirit-beings have the capacity to assume tangible physical form. Yet, occult history testifies that this is the case. In missionary lands, tales are told of demon spirits that materialize and seek to inflict bodily injury upon their victims, often biting, striking, or choking humans. These phenomena are seldom observed because God has severely restricted such activity. Satan's power, one must remember, is limited to the sphere of influence in which God by His greater power allows the devil to operate for a season. It should be pointed out that a materialized demon is normally not visible to the naked eye. By materialization, it is meant that a tangible form is assumed and the demon can be "felt" during the experience of incubus. Furthermore, literal impregnation is not possible. *Rosemary's Baby* is, after all, pure fantasy. Christ who has come to save men will allow only redeemable beings to assume human form. Satan's power is thus limited to the act of intercourse without the ability to conceive a life form. Creation is the sole perogative of God.

For those who seek a biblical illustration of incubus there is the theological possibility of interpreting Genesis 6:1-4 in this manner. I am not suggesting that such an allegory is absolute but would like to present the plausibility of arguments in its favor. The phrase in verse two "sons of God," which throughout Scripture refers to angels, seems to indicate a distinction between them and the "daughters of men." It may well be that these "sons of God" were fallen angels who, as instruments of Satan, sought to thwart God's plan of salvation by destroying the purity of the

Adamic line, producing a mongrel progeny, part demon and part human. This would certainly explain the giant offspring.

The phrase "also after that" (which may refer to that period following the Flood) would additionally explain the existence of giants after the deluge as being a result of incubus relations. With this in mind, we can see that the purpose of the Flood may have been for God to completely destroy corrupted mankind, except for the purity of the Adamic line found in Noah and his sons. When Satan recognized that God had promised there would not be another Flood cataclysm to destroy the earth, he may have attempted this diabolical scheme once again. This could explain why God commanded Israel to kill all the inhabitants, including children, of the lands that they entered into. To suggest that the "sons of God" is in reference to sons of Seth, the godly line, is not plausible since the "daughters of men" (supposedly the line of Cain) were all killed by the flood and there would have been no daughters of Cain to marry after the Flood.

Two nagging questions are raised by this hypothesis. Demons are spirit beings. To support this theory, it would be necessary for them to create physical bodies capable of impregnation through sexual intercourse. Furthermore, if such were possible both before and after the Flood, when did such activity cease and why is incubus possible today only without impregnation? Perhaps an answer may be found in Jude 6, 7 and 2 Peter 2:4. If we interpret these Scriptures as refering to the fallen angels who were the "sons of God" in Genesis 6 it might be that their judgment for this sin is their current imprisonment in chains. Whereas other demons are free to roam about, these demons are confined awaiting the day of judgment. Seeing their example and desiring to remain free in activity, perhaps demons today refrain from intercourse impregnation and thus not incur the same judgment of imprisonment that the fallen angels of Genesis 6 did.

The reader will have to come to his own conclusions. This theory has been set forth as only one of several possible explanations regarding the existence of giants and mutated offspring in the Old Testament. Whether or not this passage of Scripture is in reference to incubus, such cohabitation (without conception) is possible today. Examples are numerous. The following story regards one of several encounters we have had with those engaged in this form of sexual perversion.

At the conclusion of a large youth rally I was conversing with some of the young people who came to question me about various remarks in my message. I counseled with them, giving special attention to the ones who, by the nature of their questions, indicated that they probably did not know Christ as their personal Savior. My comments sought to point them to the reality of my faith in Christ and share with them the scriptural basis for coming to know the Lord. It was then that a voice spoke up out of the midst of the group, "I don't believe in God. I am an atheist."

My attention was drawn to a short, blonde-haired girl who looked to be about fifteen. She was dressed in a blouse with slacks that had a slit up one leg all the way to the thigh. She stood there with a rather sultry and defiant gaze and said again, "There's no God. How do you know there is a God? I don't believe it; I'm an atheist."

Normally I would have ignored such a remark of obvious antagonism. At first my reaction was to not pay any attention and to continue speaking with those who seemed to be more sincerely interested in talking about the things of the Lord. But something, (I know now it was the Spirit of God) said within me, "This girl needs help."

I turned to the young lady and said, "Do you really mean that? You actually don't believe there is a God?"

"Yes," she replied. "I don't believe in your Jesus."

"Would you step aside with me for a few moments to talk?" I asked.

She nodded yes and I beckoned for her to come apart from the others so that I could converse with her more directly without interference.

"If you don't believe in God," I said, "do you believe in the devil?"

"Yes!" she answered, a smirking, leering smile crossing her lips.

"Why do you believe in the devil?" I asked.

Her eyes grew intense. "Because I've felt him," she answered.

"What do you mean by that?" I inquired.

"I've given my body to him in sexual relationship. I'm married to the devil," was her reply.

I was taken back at first with her answer. I wondered to myself if I could actually be encountering a case of incubus. Her obvious sincerity sent chills up my spine as I realized that she was more than just another impudent teen-ager.

"I'd like to talk with you for a few moments. Would you step into another room where we could spend a few moments in prayer and counsel?" I suggested.

She nodded with a flippancy that seemed to almost be a challenge, as if to say, "Why not, I'm not afraid of you."

I stepped aside to one of the young people there and asked him to go to the back of the church and get my wife Kathy to join us. Not only did I not want to counsel alone with this young lady but I knew that I was going to need prayerful support throughout the ordeal if indeed I was facing a genuine case of incubus.

We entered a Sunday school classroom and I told the young lady to be seated. I picked up a chair and sat it exactly opposite this teen-age atheist. She told me her name was "Ann" (a pseudonym used for the purposes of this story) and began to describe her sexual relationships with the materialized demon spirit. Every detail was glorified as she told of her "marriage" to the devil. Ann knew she needed help but seemed to be indifferent in her attitude. It was as if a mood of hopeless despair had gripped her. Sometimes she stared blankly into space and at other times she was intensely antagonistic. I tried to get her to pray and to seek God's help. She refused and was careful to avoid ever saying the name of Jesus. If this were just another teen-ager with some wild story, what a prank it would be to get me to believe such a fantastic tale only to say afterwards that it had been a joke all the time.

132

"You're not serious, are you, Ann?" I prodded her.

She became quite angry and belligerent at the thought that I might not believe her. I wanted to be certain that this was not just a case of delusion or merely a grasp at attention by unveiling such intimate details of her sexual life. But the more that I conversed with Ann the more that I became convinced this was a desperate situation—one that was going to necessitate a confrontation with hell.

Bowing my head for a moment, I prayed, "Lord, I don't want to make a mistake. I know how dangerous it is to suspect demon possession and then later to be wrong and create a feeling of paranoia. Jesus, help me. Give me the wisdom to know what to do." In silence, I meditated for a moment and prayed to find God's direction.

Finally, I knew what had to be done. "Ann, I am not going to talk to you anymore," I said, "I'm going to talk to the power that is controlling you."

"Demon, I command in the name of Jesus that you identify yourself," I demanded.

The look that came across Ann's countenance left no more questions in my mind. She immediately entered a trance state. Her face became contorted, her body stiffened, and a fiendishly defiant gaze shot forth from her eyes. From deep within her body came a guttural reply. "Yes," the voice answered sarcastically, "What do you want?"

I turned to my wife, who is Canadian. Being familiar with the English accent, she was almost in a state of shock. The voice that we heard was not Ann's; it was the voice of a demon. It spoke forth with a most beautifully eloquent and perfectly enunicated British accent that no actress could have ever mimicked. Hell had actually answered.

"What is your name, demon?" I asked.

It refused to tell and in belligerency tried to push the question aside. Three more times I demanded to know the name of the demon.

Finally the voice answered again through Ann's vocal chords in that same perfectly spoken British accent. "Miss Love" was the reply.

I knew that "Miss Love" was not the real name but only a pseudonym that the demon was using to conceal its true identity. I could have gone ahead at that time to pin the demon down as to its exact name but I felt that it was best to continue on to learn more of the situation and for practical purposes referred to the demon as "Miss Love." It's interesting to note that the demon chose to lie from the start by concealing its true identity.

Curious as to its vocal inflection, I spoke to the demon again. "That's a British accent, isn't it? Are you a British demon?"

"Yes," was the answer from Miss Love, "I've inhabited many British subjects, including Queen Elizabeth I."

I wasn't sure whether or not the statement of inhabiting Queen Elizabeth was a matter of fact or merely an egotistical claim. Whatever the case, one point is obvious: a possessed person who dies no longer provides a vessel. At death the demon goes elsewhere. Demon spirits do not die but may continually inhabit those who yield to them throughout the centuries. It is entirely possible this demon could have inhabited Queen Elizabeth I or any other number of personages in times past.

I was anxious to know if what Ann had told me was the truth. "Is it true that you own Ann's body and have engaged in sexual relationships with her?" I asked.

The affirmative response sobered me even more. "I'm going to claim Ann for Christ," I informed Miss Love.

The demon insisted that I could not have her. I knew the only way that the battle could be won would be for Ann to exert her will. She was possessed but while out of the trance state I hoped to be able to convince her to exercise her volition and refuse the demon control over her life.

"Miss Love," I said, "I am not going to talk to you now. I want Ann to answer."

Immediately, the demonic look left her face and a somewhat passive gaze came over her. "Ann," I said, "I know what you are telling me is the truth, but you can be free. I'm going to pray with you and try to help you. You are possessed by a demon, but with God's help I can cast it out. I can't do it without you. We must have the exercise of your free will. You have to help us."

I could tell at that moment that the demon was struggling for the control of Ann's body. She tensed as I grasped her hands and struggled to hold her still. It seemed as if the demon was thrusting about inside of her.

Finally she spoke. "It's no use. I'm married and Miss Love owns my body."

I noticed a small gold cross hanging around her neck. "You have no right to wear that cross," I said, "if you claim to be married to the devil."

She took the cross loose from around her neck and started to throw it at me. I grabbed her hands and held on as she shook violently. The cross slipped out of her grasp and fell to the floor.

I was thankful that although the demon did possess her it was not a case of absolute, total dominance. She was able to come out of the demon trance and could speak somewhat for herself, though her will was extremely vulnerable to the wishes of the demon.

Ann rose to her feet and walked about the room in despair. She wanted to help, but the demon had convinced her that there was no way out.

"I want to be free but I can't be free," she cried. A slight pause followed and then she reversed herself. "No, on second thought, I don't want to be free."

Not knowing what to do, I again bowed by head for a moment to pray. Seldom have I ever had God speak to my heart so clearly with divine wisdom as at that moment. A split second later I found myself addressing the demon. "Miss Love I want to talk to you."

Once again that hideous look came across Ann's face. I continued, "You're going to kill Ann, aren't you?" I had no idea what made me say it except that God had given me supernatural knowledge. It was something that only God could have shown me.

"Yes," the demon answered, "I'm going to kill Ann."

"How?" I demanded.

The demon hedged for a few moments, not wanting to answer me. Finally my persistence paid. "Ann will hang herself from a tree," was the verdict.

"Does Ann know this?" I asked.

136

"Yes," the demon answered.

"Ann, I want to speak to you again."

That awful look faded from her face and she almost seemed her natural self. "I have just spoken with Miss Love," I said. "Do you know what is going to happen to you? Do you know what the demon is going to do to you?"

"I am going to kill myself. You see, I have to die on a cross like Jesus," she replied.

Ann didn't understand how her death would be brought about. She didn't know that the way she would emulate the death of Christ would be for the demon to cause her to hang herself. Again I spoke to Miss Love and inquired as to when this would happen. The demon said that it was going to kill Ann as soon as possible. There was no doubt in my mind as to how strategic our meeting was. The mercy of God had sent us to Ann, perhaps as the last chance before her own life was suicidally claimed.

Realizing how desperate the situation was, I began to plead more earnestly with Ann. Intermittently she would look up at the large clock hanging from the wall. It seemed the more we talked the more she somehow mustered the strength of her will and wanted to be free from the power that controlled her. She told me that whatever I did I had to do by twelve o'clock because, in her words, "terrible things happen after midnight and you have to help me before then."

I knew that this was not true. She could receive help no matter what the time was, but somehow the demon was using the midnight hour to intimidate her. Apparently the demon was trying to get us to rush things or to believe that once the midnight hour was past there would be no other way out for Ann. The more I spoke the more I began to see a slight glimmer of hope that the victory could be won. I determined to make it known once and for all to the demon that there was no way that we were going to back down.

I addressed Miss Love again. "You might as well know that we claim Ann for Christ. You cannot have her body and you do not own her. Through the power in the name of Jesus we are going to defeat you."

The demon began to scream and vent its anger upon me. "What right do you have to tell me what to do? I remember you before you were saved. I know the kind of life you lived before you became a Christian. I saw you. I know the things you did. What right do you, a sinner, have to tell me what to do? You have no power; I know how you lived, and you have no right to demand anything of me."

Never in my entire ministry have I experienced a moment when I recognized more how wonderful the transforming mercy of Christ can be. I looked firmly into the eyes of Ann. Yet, they were not Ann's eyes—they were the eyes of the demon who possessed her. I knew that I was staring into hell itself, for I saw hell staring back at me. With calmness, composure, a slight smile on my lips, and with joy in my heart I answered, "Yes, it is true there were many years I lived in sin, many years when I did not serve Christ. But you demon of hell, there is one thing that I want you to know. The blood of Jesus Christ has covered my past. It has washed away my sins. In God's sight these

138

things are forgotten, and in the mercy, grace, and cleansing power of the blood of Jesus, on His merit alone, I have every right to confront you. I command you in the name of Jesus to shut your mouth."

The voice of the demon was stilled and it stopped its screaming. It knew the power in the name and the blood of Christ. There was no answer it could give. At that name, as Paul told us in Philippians 2:9,10, the devils themselves must bow.

I heard a sound and looked over my shoulder. The room had been locked but the church janitor, not knowing what was going on inside, had used his master key to open the door and came in. The hour was late, he told us, and it was nearly midnight. He wondered if it would be possible for us to leave and go elsewhere for our prayer and counseling.

I walked out into a lobby area with Ann and Kathy. As we stepped outside I saw that several of Ann's friends as well as others were there. I didn't know what to do. The hour was late and they were waiting to take her home. It seemed to be a hopeless situation, and I saw no way out of it unless Ann would somehow exercise her will to be free. We passed her friends and walked toward where the youth pastor from the church she attended was standing. Suddenly she collapsed sobbing in his arms. I recognized that this was the first time any sign of emotion had ever been expressed from her.

She cried for a moment, and then weeping turned to me. "Please, Mr. Larson, you've got to help me," she said.

Somehow the power of the Holy Spirit was fighting an unseen battle and the power of the demon was wearing down. Even when the demon was not speaking audibly through her vocal cords and she was out of the complete trance state, she still was in a semitrance condition. She did not know entirely what was going on, and although she was not totally controlled she was at least demonically subjected to the point that she could not bring herself to exercise her free will.

What happened next I have absolutely no explanation for. I cannot explain it theologically, for it seems to refute what one would expect from a fallen angel. I was shocked as I looked into Ann's eyes and saw them take on the demon expression. Then the voice spoke: "If you really want to help Ann, if you really want her to be free, take her to your motel room and there with a Bible show her, step by step, the scriptural plan of salvation from the Word of God."

I was stunned. Was the demon actually telling me how to cast himself out? That was what was happening. I still cannot figure out why except to say that, somehow, the sovereign grace of God intervened and made the demon say what it said. At that moment I knew victory could be won and it could be won through the power of the Word of God.

I asked Ann's pastor and the others who were present if it would be all right for us to take her to our motel room and counsel with her further. They said that it would be fine, and we appointed a time at which they could return to pick her up. I requested that another minister friend come with us.

On the way to the motel the demon began to subject Ann and kept her in constant fear that the midnight hour would pass and that she could not be helped from then on.

While we were making the trip the demon also tried an old trick that I had heard from others who had counseled with demon possession. The demon attempted to bring a "sleep" upon Ann to feign fatigue. I knew what was happening and would not allow Ann to slumber. I shook her and gently slapped her face to stir her out of her lethargy. As I did, the voice within her laughed mockingly as if to say, "This isn't real sleep. I'm just trying to fool you, but I see that it hasn't done any good." I knew that the best way to keep her awake and to combat the demon activity would be with God's Word. Throughout the entire trip of twenty minutes I quoted Scriptures, one after another. The Word of God is powerful, more powerful than a two-edged sword. It was sufficient to keep Ann awake and in her right mind.

Finally we arrived at the motel. We went inside and I had Ann seated in a comfortable chair facing where I sat. As we began to converse it was apparent that the demon was setting up its defenses once again. The period of passiveness that had entered the mood of Ann passed. She again became quite belligerent. Now was the time, I determined, to apply the effectiveness of God's Word.

Taking my Bible, I showed Ann the plan of salvation from the Scriptures, taking her step by step and asking that she read each Scripture, being sure that she understood its meaning. When this was completed and God's Word had done it work, I addressed the demon.

"You are defeated," I insisted. "I am now going to claim Ann's body and soul for Jesus Christ."

The demon seemed intent on trying to argue and tried to prolong the situation as long as possible. He knew that he was defeated and that there was no way that his dominance of Ann's life could be maintained. Earlier, back at the church, the demon had seemed very nasty and violently offensive. Now, knowing that he was defeated, the demon became almost congenial and conversational. What he said next was both shocking and informative.

(I should explain that, following the example of our Lord, one does not normally allow a demon to speak except to obtain the necessary information to facilitate the exorcism procedure. Now that I was certain of victory over this demon, however, I felt impressed by the Holy Spirit to allow it to speak.)

"This is not the first time we've met," the demon said. "I know you and I have followed you many places about the country before."

"Did you hear what I said tonight," I asked, "when I spoke to the young people about the dangers of hard-rock music and specifically the way in which demon possession and demon influence can be involved with rock music?"

"Yes," the demon answered. "What you said was true, every word of it."

The demon then proceeded to taunt me, "I saw the young people come forward at your invitation. I saw the dedications to God that they made. But remember, when they go back to their churches many of them will sing my songs; even

142

the churches will sing my songs and I will deceive even the elect."

As I heard this revelation I wondered if anyone would believe it. I was glad that my wife and minister friend were present too. To have the demon substantiate my fears regarding the use of rock music in the church seemed like an easily fabricated story to support one's position. Demons can and do lic. Many times throughout the night in conversation this demon had lied. But it is always easy to discern when a demon is telling the truth. There is a sincerity and fervency with which it speaks when it is saying something that it believes and wants communicated. There could be no doubt but that this demon believed what I said to be true and intended to use certain rock music forms to deceive the leadership in some churches.

The demon was not finished and went on. "Even though you spoke the truth, remember also, I am in all types of music—country and western, classical, popular, and rock. If you want to know where to find me the most look for me in the words, in the ideas and philosophies expressed in the songs; you will find me."

That was a statement that I could heartily agree with. In the past many people have accused me of singling out rock music in my books and lectures as being the only instrument and tool of Satan. That simply is not so. As I have often said, there are many other music forms that in their lyrical content are just as dangerous to Christian conduct because of the immorality expressed in the words.

Since the demon was in a talkative mood and

143

obviously intent upon glorifying his works and purposes, I asked, "Are there any particular rock groups that you would like to mention as being under demon influence?"

The demon smiled through the face of Ann and proceeded to speak. "Alice Cooper is demon possessed. We make him get on the floor and make love to that snake. On one occasion we made him slit the neck of the snake and drink its cold, uncoagulated blood."

The voice went on to explain several other groups such as Black Sabbath that it inhabited and inspired. After the list the demon said, "Would you like to know something else about the death of Janis Joplin?"

I said that I would, and the demon then proceeded to tell me a most amazing story. The newspapers reported that Miss Joplin had died of an overdose of heroin. From the journalistic accounts it appeared as if her death might have come about as a result of an accidental overdose. I talked with some who had seen Janis when she was discovered dead in the motel room and they attested to the fact that her face was battered beyond recognition. The supposition was that she had hit the nightstand rolling off the bed and disfigured and bloodied her face. The demon had another story.

"Janis Joplin did not die as the result of an accident," the voice said. "She knew exactly what she was doing and it was not heroin in the hypodermic syringe. In fact, there were two needles. Janis walked into that motel room and shoved both needles into her arms. One contained a form of liquid cement and the other a high grade of LSD. Then, under our inspiration, she looked into a mirror. With a razor blade and her fingernails she ripped and tore the flesh on her face to pieces until she collapsed in a pool of her own flesh and blood." The demon seemed to enjoy every little detail and smiled confidently as it spoke.

The reader may wonder whether or not to accept such an account. Do not demons lie? Yes, but as I said before, you can usually tell when they are. This demon meant every word of what it said. The reader can decide whether or not to accept its credibility, but I can firmly attest that there is no doubt in my mind that the demon was speaking the truth. That there should be a discrepancy between this story and the story told by the newspaper account is not surprising, since one could not expect those involved with Miss Joplin to accept a story such as this detailing the final moments of her life.

Back at the church, I'd been amazed that the demon should explain to me the way in which he could be defeated, by taking Ann scripturally through the Bible. What the demon said next baffled me more.

Demons are fallen angels without hope. Scripture plainly shows that their eternal destiny is the lake of fire. There is no way a demon can be saved. These fallen spirits have no hope of redemption. They are depraved, lewd, and sinful beyond comprehension. Their diabolic purposes are to destroy men, and throughout history they have been associated with the most vile acts of murder and perversion. I was shocked, therefore, to hear the demon's next statement.

"Go," the demon said, "to Alice Cooper, Black Sabbath, and the other rock groups that I have told you about and tell them about your Jesus so that they don't have to go to the place that I am going to have to go."

Imagine that. An unregenerate, hopelessly lost, debased spirit not wanting anyone to have to suffer the consequences of its sin. Even though this same demon had undoubtedly possessed, destroyed, and consigned to eternal punishment scores of lives, in this one moment of defeat, a tinge of remorse crossed its character. Reprobate as it was, it understood its horrible destiny and did not want anyone else to have to go there.

At this point Miss Love was quite passive and cooperative. I addressed her. "Do you know now that you are defeated?"

The demon nodded and replied in the affirmative.

"In just a moment I am going to exorcise you through the power in the name of Jesus and cast you into outer darkness. Is there anything you would like to say before you are cast out?"

A slight gleam came into the eyes of Ann through the influence of the demon and the voice said, "Yes, get me a copy of the lyrics of *Jesus Christ Superstar*. I inspired it and I want to show you the songs that I am most proud of."

I would like to remind the reader at this point that the rock opera *Jesus Christ Superstar* was written in Great Britain by two Englishmen. One is an atheist and the other an agnostic. Both men admit that they do not believe in Christ and said their intentions in the rock opera were to "present him as a man, not as a God." Robert Stigwood,

146

the producer and mastermind behind *Superstar,* has also been claimed by some to be a rather infamous homosexual. It is he, perhaps more than the composers, who is responsible for the worldwide popularity of *Jesus Christ Superstar.* I likewise remind the reader again that this demon claimed to be a British demon inhabiting British subjects. The correlation should be obvious.

At the church that night I had spoken with reference to the rock opera *Jesus Christ Superstar* and illustrated to the audience a copy of the souvenir program from the live production. The program contains the lyrics of all of the songs. I motioned for Kathy to get the program from my briefcase and bring it to us. She did and I handed it to Ann. Possessing and controlling the body, the mind, and vocal chords of Ann, the demon picked up the souvenir program and opened its pages. Turning from song to song, it smiled and pointed out the lyrics of which it was most proud. Of particular pride were the songs sung by Judas.

I looked the demon in the eye and said, " 'Miss Love' is not your real name, is it?"

The demon smiled. "No," it said.

"In the name of Jesus I command you, tell me your real identity."

"If you want to know who I really am," the voice answered, "read in the Bible the thirteenth chapter of Revelation."

I turned the pages of Scripture and began to read at the first verse: "And I stood upon the sand of the sea and saw a beast rise up out of the sea, having seven heads and ten horns, and upon his horns ten crowns, and upon his head the name of blasphemy."

"Blasphemy," I said. "So that's your real name."

A hideous smile curled across the lips of this young lady as the voice said, "Yes, my real name is Blasphemy."

Then without the slightest glance at the Bible which I was holding, the voice took up at verse two, and from the King James Version quoted verbatim remaining verses from Revelation chapter thirteen. This was incontestable proof, if anyone would have desired any, that none of this was staged. There is no way that Ann could have fooled us, first of all by mimicking the British accent, and finally by perfectly quoting such a rather obscure passage of Scripture.

It was then that the rite of exorcism began. I soon discovered that Blasphemy, though the main demon, was not the only demon that possessed Ann. There were seven in all, and we required that each demon identify itself by name. The sequence of casting them out was commenced by having each demon speak audibly and pronounce its own doom.

"I want you to repeat after me," I said to the first demon identified as Lust, "the following words, 'I, the demon of Lust, come out of Ann in the name of Jesus and consign myself to outer darkness.' "

The first demon began to speak and then stopped declaring, "I can't say the name of J—, I mean, that name." The demon slightly smirked and realized that it had tripped itself up. It really could say the name of Jesus and almost did, but caught itself. My wife later said this again was ab-solute proof, convincing her that this never could

148

have been acted out and was in reality a demon spirit speaking.

The demon was finally made to pronounce the name of Jesus and seal its own doom. Each demon subsequently followed the same process of exorcism. On several occasions the demon would give a false name. Each time, God graciously allowed us to discern this error and to pin the demon down, making it state its real name. One demon identified itself as Monica (a fictious name I have used to hide her real name). I demanded to know from the demon why it had chosen this name, and it explained that Monica was the name of Ann's neighbor girlfriend who had gotten her involved in witchcraft. At that time I addressed Ann directly, stating to her that she could not have a demon of another person inhabiting her. I wanted to know more about Monica, and Ann explained that it was the Ouija board and seances of Monica that drew her into satanic rituals and ultimately led to incubus.

We persisted to find the real name of the Monica demon and cast it out as well. Finally, the seventh demon, Blasphemy, came forth.

When the last demon exited, there could be no doubt that victory had been won; it was apparent all over Ann's face. Her head drooped, and a calm, serene, and composed gaze came across her face. It was the first time that we had seen the *real* Ann. She started herself, jerked slightly, and looked up.

"Where am I?" she asked. "What has been going on?"

It was obvious that even when she spoke for herself and was not under total demon possession, she still had been in a trance-like state. In fact, four hours had passed since she first approached me back at the church, and she had no recollection whatsoever of what had transpired in the interim period. As we talked with her, for a moment she began unconsciously to finger the neckline of her blouse and run her hand across her throat. I wondered what she was doing at first until finally she said, "Where is my necklace?"

She did not even remember taking off her necklace to throw it away. I reached into my pocket and handed it to her. She smiled. What a beautiful smile it was. Just the kind of smile one would have expected to come from the face of a fifteen-year-old teen-ager. It was the first time that we had seen *that* look. There could be no doubt about it; Ann was free!

"Ann," I said. "You have been freed from these powers that have bound your life. Now will you receive Christ as your Savior?"

Ann smiled again and nodded her head. I shared with her a few thoughts about salvation and quoted a few remaining Scriptures. Then I led her in a sinner's prayer. She prayed after me and casually, without thought, invoked the name of Jesus.

Jesus! She actually said that name. To think that for four hours she was not able to say the name of Christ and that now she calmly and reverently whispered His name. I could not help but think how these demons in the blackness of outer darkness must be cringing to hear that name, Jesus. I don't know that I have ever heard Christ's name spoken so sweetly and beautifully before. I have never before in my life recognized more the power and authority that is found in that name, the name of Jesus.

By now it was nearly two-thirty. Ann was concerned about contacting her parents and was worried that they might not know where she was. I did not want to prolong matters but spent a few moments counseling her about the importance of attending church and being faithful to the things of God. She had been attending church and in fact had sung in the youth choir but had never accepted Christ as her personal Savior.

I rejoice in knowing that Ann was rescued. I have new faith in the power of Christ's blood and in the efficacy of His atonement. More than ever I am convinced that productions such as *Superstar* are conceived in the mind of Satan. We must determine to fight these active agents of the enemy and not fear speaking out against them.

One point is a particular source of rejoicing. When Jesus cast the devils out of the demoniac of the Gadarenes, the demons requested to go into a herd of swine. Why? By reentering another life-form, their perpetuity of possession would be assured. Demons must always be cast into outer darkness and be bound by the word of authority in the name of Jesus. There is no way back from there. Christ, however, fooled that legion of devils by allowing them to enter the herd of swine. Their attempt at possessive perpetuity was foiled when the swine ran down a steep place and were drowned in the sea.

Had we never encountered Ann, that demon Blasphemy would have been free to possess other lives in the future. Its diabolical purposes in inspiring *Superstar* would have perhaps found vent in the inspiration of other productions designed to discredit the reality of Christ. Now it is bound and there is no way back.

I cannot speculate how many other demons may have helped to inspire *Superstar* and other similar productions. There is no way of knowing. I do believe, however as the result of victory in Ann's life, the ultimate effect of *Jesus Christ Superstar* has been diminished. It may well be that we were the instruments of God to circumvent these purposes of Satan in these last days. I am not suggesting that there will never be another production, musical or otherwise, based upon blasphemy. I am only saying that this was one step in thwarting Satan's attack. How we thank God that He gave us the wisdom and power through His name to bind this evil force.

My heart grieves for those preachers and Christian leaders who serve as apologists for the religious blasphemy of *Jesus Christ Superstar* and similar productions. They will someday be held accountable before God. I pray that through the telling of this story you the reader will become more determined to take a stand against inroads that Satan has made in the Church and will speak forcibly wherever your voice may be heard. Remember, there are other Anns who need help.

7

The God of Hellfire

Do you think that it is possible for a man to walk on fire without getting burned? Could he hold white-hot coals in his hands without so much as getting a blister? Impossible, you say! With my own eyes I have seen such feat—exhibitions of heathen, satanic power.

In his pop hit "American Pie," Don McLean metaphorically described a Rolling Stones performance. Alluding to their satanic image, McLean wrote: "Fire is the devil's only friend,/... the flames climbed high into the night/to light the sacrificial light/I saw Satan laughing with delight . . . ." The fusion of satanic images and fire in "American Pie" is rather reminiscent of Arthur Brown, one of the most satanic rock personalities. Brown, who used to bill his act as "The Crazy

World of Arthur Brown," was one of the forerunners of of theatric stage-rock that is so much a part of performances today by people such as Alice Cooper. Brown descended upon the stage in a freaky costume looking very much like a warlock. With red flames and smoke bombs on stage, each performance crescendoed to a demonic climax. It was then that Brown would sing his hit "The God of Hellfire," in which he declared, "I am the god of hellfire and you're going to burn, burn, burn."

I will not take the reader through an extensive analysis of the significance regarding the relationship between Lucifer and fire. Scripture shows plainly that hell is a place of fire and that the eventual destination of Satan and his cohorts is "the lake of fire" (Revelation 19:20). The parable that Christ told in the sixteenth chapter of Luke regarding the rich man illustrates that such references are literal. This man craved a drop of water to cool his tongue, a request that would not have been necessary were the biblical references to hellfire only metaphors. The demonic ritual of fire-walking is perhaps the most lucid expression of Satan's relationship to fire. For a few moments, come with me to the beautiful South Pacific island of Fiji to observe this pagan rite.

Fiji is a newly independent nation consisting of 800 islands in the Pacific east of Australia. It is a land of sugar cane, coral reefs, and waving palm trees. The majority of the people live on the main island of Viti Levu, where most of the population is comprised of dark-skinned native Fijians. During the nineteenth century, the British, who were then in control of the island, imported thousands of East Indian laborers. Today nearly one-half of the population of Fiji is of Indian descent. The natives are at least nominally Christianized, but the Indians brought with them the religion of their homeland, Hinduism. They still practice it with a fervency unmatched in some places in India. Fire-walking is an example.

The black Fijians also practice fire-walking. A certain tribe from a neighboring island journeys once every two weeks to the site of a plush resort hotel. There before the assembled tourists who pay four dollars each, the fire-walking ritual is carried out with a great deal of pomp and drama. The Fijian fire-walk is a stroll upon a circular pit that is filled with large stones which have been superheated until they become red hot. I have seen this ritual and must confess that I am not positive as to what extent Satan does play a role. Certainly the accompanying theatrics make one suspicious as to whether or not trickery may be partially involved. I am convinced that the power of Satan does aid their efforts but would not be so dogmatic as to say that each Fijian fire-walker is completely possessed of demon spirits. There appears to be a lack of direct religious devotion to any occult power and a spirit of gaiety makes the whole scene more tourist-appeasing than idol-appeasing. I cannot say the same for the Hindu fire-walk. Its seriousness and devotion to satanic powers is apparent from the beginning to conclusion of the entire ritual.

In India, fire-walking has been outlawed in most places, but it still flourishes on Fiji. It was quite by "accident" that we came upon this Hindu ceremony, because it takes place only once a year at a special religious festival. My wife and I were browsing one day in a tourist shop in the port city of Nandi. I was casually discussing the fire-walk with several storekeepers. Much to my amazement, one young man told me that in two days there would be a fire-walking ceremony nearby. One eighteen-year-old clerk told me that he had fire-walked and proudly described the experience, including the piercing of his cheeks and tongue with spikes. "There was no blood shed," he said, "and I didn't even know what was going on. I was in a trance the whole time. God gave me the power to undergo this ordeal." As I stood listening intently to this young man it was astounding to consider that as personable and friendly as he was, he had to have been demonically possessed and controlled during his fire-walk experience. I inquired from him as to some specifics regarding the ceremony and what the possibility would be of our attending it. He told me that, unlike the Fijian ceremony, the Hindu fire-walk ritual is not publicized for tourist observation. To the Indians, this is a very sacred time and one not to be demeaned by commercialization. He felt that it would be possible for me to see the ceremony and suggested that I visit the headquarters temple to make sure. With directions in hand I left the store to drive to the nearby temple to check on my chances of observing the rite of walking on fire.

After a journey of some distance on an infrequently traveled dirt road we came upon a small temple located in the middle of a field about the size of a football stadium. We parked the car and walked near the temple. Several ladies were overseeing the grounds that day and none of them

156

could speak English. One of them walked to a nearby house which, I learned later, belonged to the temple manager. Soon there came to greet us his teen-age daughter, who spoke fluent English.

The young lady informed us that the fire-walking ceremony would definitely take place here. She filled us in on many of the circumstances surrounding it, explaining various details regarding the preparation for the fire-walk. Then, she asked if I would like to step inside and view the idol that gives men such power. I consented.

We entered the small temple and she proudly pointed to a crudely carved wooden idol about three feet high. The idol's name, I was informed, is Draupati. Its hands were carved in an outstretched position with the palms up. The eyes were of particular significance. They were oversized, seeming to stare with a life-like intensity. That piercing gaze became more evident when the girl pulled back a thin veil that had covered its face. Lying about the idol were a number of pictures representing various incarnations of the Hindu godhead. Sensing that I was desirous to know more about the ritual, she was extremely helpful in volunteering a brief but concise explanation.

"The preparation for the ritual takes seven days," she explained, "and during that time the fire-walk devotees walk from home to home in the vicinity. They sing, offer prayers, and bless each home they come to. During this period there is a fast when each fire-walker must abstain from meats and women."

She went on to point out that the reason for the presence of so many ladies at the temple was that the fire-walk was being sponsored by the

Women's Auxiliary. My interest heightened as she continued describing the miracle signs that confirm the fact that there would be no danger for the devotees.

"Before each man walks on the fire, he must kneel and pray in front of the idol of the goddess Draupati," she stated. "A garland of flowers about this size" (she held her hands about eight inches apart) "will be placed on the head of the idol. Each devotee will pray with his hands outstretched. If he is to walk, the garland will lift into the air and drop into his hands."

Levitation!—that ancient black art of satanic manifestation had its roots in Hindu religious practices. How disturbed it made me feel to hear this explanation and to know that many young people, even Christians, casually practice this phenomenon. I couldn't help but think of these stories I had heard of parties where people were lifted from the floor or a chair on the fingertips of four or five of their friends. But here in Fiji, the working of Satan that performs such a feat is not considered a game. It is serious business to these people and a sign of the power of their goddess.

"What happens if the garland doesn't lift into the air and drop into the hands of the devotee?" I asked.

"It's the fault of the devotee. He has probably not been properly purified," she answered. "I have known this to happen. When it does, all of the devotees gather for prayer. The priest beats them until the unpurified one confesses the truth. One time a devotee had incorrectly drunk the holy water solution that fire-walkers must drink before the ritual. After beating him he confessed and

158

then drank it properly. When he knelt before the idol the next time, the garland lifted into the air."

My temple tour guide invited me to walk on the flaming coals. She added, however, that my condition for doing so would be to pray in devotion to the idol. Obviously, I declined.

I began to quiz her more specifically about the fire-walking and mentioned the fact that the native Fijians walk on fire too. To my question as to why she believed her goddess since its miracle power could be duplicated by the Fijians, she responded with a somewhat incredulous look. She had never thought about the possibility of other gods having such power. She did counter my inquiry by pointing out that the Fijians walk on super-heated stones. The Hindus, she explained, actually walk on the flaming coals themselves which are much hotter. When I inquired further as to what her reaction would be if I prayed to my God to keep the garland from falling, she again looked rather dumbfounded. This said something to me about the Hindu religious mentality. They seem to blindly accept the supernatural abilities of their gods and never consider the possibility that this might not be a valid criterion for establishing spiritual truth.

I looked outside to where my wife was standing and saw that she appeared fidgety. Perhaps she thought I might be tempted to take seriously the young lady's invitation to walk on the fire. I later assured her this was not the case.

We stepped back outside, and from the front door of the temple I looked straight ahead toward the fire-walk area. A freshly dug pit was located in the center of the temple grounds. It was ap-

159

proximately twenty feet long, about four feet wide, and six to eight inches deep. Next to the pit was a pile of lumber and firewood—fifteen tons of it. The temple manager's daughter told me that if I would like to speak personally with some of the fire-walkers I could do so that night when they gathered. I thanked her for her time and walked back to our car.

Before driving off I stopped to gaze at the beautiful scenery around us. A flag was waving in the stiff breeze that tossed the graceful palm trees about. The serenity of my surroundings seemed ill-suited for such a dramatic display in evidence of demonic powers. In forty-eight hours the scene that I looked upon would be transformed into satanic "holy ground."

As I thought back upon the comments of the temple manager's daughter, I had to admit I never realized the full potential of Satan's power. The levitation of the flower garland was not the only satanic feat she had described. The priest, I was told, would be the first to step out onto the coals. Before the others walked he would throw the garland into the flames. If it burned there would be no fire-walk. If it didn't, this would be the final miracle sign of the goddess.

"Can it be that Satan actually has power over botanical life?" I thought to myself. I remembered as well her story of a time she had seen the priest lead a sacred cow into the flames. Not even the cow was harmed, giving further false testimony to the fact that it should be worshiped as a god. I recalled the biblical story where the devils entered into a herd of swine. "Amazing," I thought. "Satan also can exercise power over animal life." I

160

drove away determined to return that night to personally converse with those who would fire-walk.

On our way back to the motel I read the announcement flyer that had been handed to me at the temple. What an irony that in ignorance they would be so proud of this pagan ritual. It read:

> There will be a thrilling fire-walk ceremony Saturday at 6:00 P.M. The prayer ceremony will be held from Tuesday to Saturday. One and all are cordially invited to attend this religious function of ours. Please do attend. This is the project of the Women's Club. We are looking forward to your good, sacred, religious function.

Later that same evening we made our way back to the fire-walking site. It was an eerie experience to say the least. A full moon was shining down out of a pitch-black sky. Since the temple area was located far off the main highway, we were in remote countryside. Imagine, if you will, the two of us Westerners in a strange land far from any city or civilized area. We stood in the middle of a field in the midst of twenty-five men who in two nights would be under such control of demon powers that they would literally walk in flames. Knowing that God was with us, we felt no fear.

I talked with several of the fire-walk devotees. The first one with whom I spoke was nineteen years of age. When I asked why he was going to walk on the fire, he said that by doing so he would be able to petition the gods for help in his studies or if any sickness should come his way. This was the third time he had walked on fire. When I asked why he was doing so again this year, he mentioned

161

that he had committed some sins the past year that would need forgiveness. By walking on the coals he believed that his god would absolve him from his sins. He admitted that some were afraid to walk on the fire but most have no fear because they are in a complete trance and do not know what happens.

My conversation with him was interrupted momentarily as I was introduced to a four-year-old child who would also walk on the fire. I couldn't help but feel an overwhelming sense of pity for this child who was bound in spiritual ignorance. His playful giggle was like that of any youngster, but he was different. Satan would also enter his body to "protect" his life from harm during the fire-walk.

I resumed my conversation with the older devotee. He again described the prayer whereby the garland of flowers lifts into the air and drops in the hands of the kneeling devotee. "Normally," he said, "it takes anywhere from one-half hour to one hour of prayer. Sometimes it takes longer." Whatever the case, they will pray the length of time necessary for the garland to levitate.

"What happens if the garland doesn't levitate?" I inquired.

He indicated that this would mean the person was not properly purified, the same story the temple manager's daughter had told me. He confirmed also that the priest would then whip them. He did add one additional piece of interesting information. If such attempts failed to reveal the unpurified culprit, one of the priests would go into a spiritualistic trance. "Then," the young man

162

said, "God will direct his mind to pinpoint the mistake."

It was obvious that these satanic powers went to great lengths to assure the devotion of those who would engage in the fire-walk ritual. "Have you ever seen anyone burned by the fire?" I asked. "How would you explain that?"

His reply: "If we get burned, that is our mistake."

The devotee went on to describe some other miraculous aspects regarding the fire-walk. "Some," he declared, "can pick up the fire and hold it in their hands without being harmed. Others put the flaming coals on their head. If we have faith no danger will come to us."

He explained further the purification process that they undergo that week. Of special importance is their prohibition against eating meat. He mentioned that if he were to touch someone unpurified he would possibly be burned during the firewalk. I joked with him about the fact that I had eaten a hamburger that day and asked him if he would shake hands with me. With a laugh he declined but went on to say that it was really quite a serious matter. Were he to touch any part of my body, his life would be in danger during the firewalk. There could be no doubt that Satan exacts a strong degree of devotion.

After I had talked with these young fire-walk devotees for over an hour and gained some information as well as their confidence, I wanted to share my faith in Christ with them. I must admit that I did so with some apprehension, considering the fact that my wife and I were the only Christian Westerners in the entire area.

I felt the best biblical way to introduce Christian truth would be to start with the story of the three Hebrew children and the fiery furnace. As I explained how the idolatrous king had cast them into the fire and how God had protected them by walking in the fire with them, he seemed anxious for me to conclude. I learned why when he in return began to share with me an identical story from Hindu mythology. I was hoping that the story of the three Hebrew children would show him that a god's ability to protect his followers from harm and fire was nothing unique. His story was of a cruel king who demanded that people worship him. He had one son who refused. The king tried unsuccessfully to kill the boy and eventually had a fire heated red-hot. He told the son to hold the fire. The child was afraid until he saw an ant crawling across the coals and said, "If an ant can do it, why not me?" The child held the fire for several hours until a god with large fingers reached down to pull him up and placed the fire on the king's chest, killing him. Duplication and counterfeit have always been Satan's plan, and this story was further evidence.

Determined not to be put off by this legend, I continued to witness about Christ. Almost immediately one of the devotees interrupted me.

"Tell me, sir," he asked, "do you believe in Jesus Christ?"

"Yes, I do," I answered.

"Well, tell me then, is it possible for a man to kill God?" he inquired further.

I hesitated for a moment and then replied, "No."

His next question told me where he was headed

164

in this line of reasoning. "Well, didn't they kill Jesus by hanging him on the Cross?"

I smiled and answered, "Yes, but He rose again from the dead!"

A puzzled look crossed the face of the young devotee. "There seems to be some confusion," he said. "Didn't they hang Jesus on a Cross and leave him there?"

With great joy I answered his question. "No, Jesus was resurrected from the dead and He is alive now with God in heaven!"

A look of astonishment filled the faces of the devotees standing about. They had heard about Christ and knew of his crucifixion—but they had never head that Jesus was a living, resurrected Savior! I thought to myself that Satan didn't mind having the world know about a crucified Savior, but he definitely did not want men to know that Jesus is also a resurrected Savior who conquered death.

With this revelation in mind, I immediately began to share with them the truth of that wonderful Easter morning when Jesus rose from the dead. At that moment, out of nowhere, I heard a voice saying to me, "Sir, are you a follower of Jesus Christ?"

A strange gentleman suddenly stepped into the group. "I know more than this young man and I would like to explain to you about our god," he proclaimed.

He said that his name was Mr. Singh and that he would like to help me better understand their religion. Though that was his stated purpose, it became apparent that he was in fact a messenger of Satan. My witnessing attempts were thwarted

165

quickly. Mr. Singh created confusion and disruption by monopolizing the entire conversation while extolling the virtures of Hinduism as the oldest and most essential religion of the world. I had no doubts that his real purpose was to disrupt my account of Christ's resurrection. It is interesting to note that the devil would allow me to speak about the death of Christ but would not permit me to proclaim that He rose again.

With a beguiling smile on his face and a copy of the *Bhagavadad-Gita* (the sacred Hindu text) in his hand, Mr. Singh went on to proclaim the inferiority of Christianity. These devotees hadn't known the true purpose of our being there, but Satan did. We had stepped into his domain and he was angry.

I saw that the conversation was getting nowhere and so politely dismissed myself. With mock cordiality Mr. Singh implored us to stay. "If you must go," he said, "please give me the pleasure of showing you around the island for the next two days."

Mr. Singh in his spiritual ignorance may have been sincere, but I was determined not to let him, a representative of hell, get in my way. "No thanks," I declined, "we've got plenty to keep us busy."

"Well, then," he said, "I'll certainly look forward to seeeing you at the fire-walk on Saturday."

I was angered at the way in which Satan had aborted my attempt to witness, but there was nothing further that could be done. I left with plans to return the next evening to see the ritual of the lighting of the firewood and the final

166

preparations to take place twenty-four hours before the fire-walk.

That night I entered into my diary an uneasy anticipation of the fire-walk day that was almost prophetic. "These Hindus don't know who we are, but Satan does. They think that when I come there Saturday night I'm coming only to observe from the standpoint of a writer. I wouldn't dare tell them who I really am and what my real pur pose is, but Satan does know. Frankly, I don't know what is going to happen."

The next night I returned to the fire-walk scene to watch the ceremony of the lighting of the fire. When we arrived, I saw that the ritual had not yet taken place and wondered what could be the significance of the music that I heard in the distance. The fire-walk devotees were sitting about the pit with hands raised in prayful devotion to the idol which had been taken out of the temple and was now sitting directly in front of the fire-walk pit. The members of the Women's Auxiliary were seated off to one side of the temple near a cement block dormitory. There they were dispensing Indian sweets to those who had come for this night of ceremony. My attention was drawn to where a large crowd was assembled near the musicians. We walked in that direction.

As we drew near I could hear laughter and shouting. "How strange," I thought, "that they should have entertainment on a night of serious religious devotion." The spectacle which I beheld as I pushed my way through the crowd was almost beyond description. The center of attention was a man about six foot three inches tall and weighing over two hundred pounds. He was dressed in women's clothing, had false breasts, make-up, and white powder with glitter sticking on his face—a transvestite. For money that the onlookers handed him in the form of a tip, he would perform some of the most graceful dancing techniques I have ever witnessed. In spite of his burly frame he twirled about in ballet-like gestures. I don't know that I have ever seen a man move with such dexterity, let alone one of such immense proportions.

At one point he walked over to an elderly gentleman and put his arms about him while kissing and fondling him. I learned later that this man in his youth had also been a transvestite dancer. Arm in arm the two of them began to dance about in the crowd-enclosed circle. With flirtatious gestures he would beckon to various men standing about.

My attention was next drawn to the musicians who were seated near the temple. Their instruments consisted of a drum, squeeze-accordian-type organ, and a long metal rod with a ring about it that one of the musicians was tapping rhythm with. I had heard this music before, but where? I searched my mind for a moment and then realized that the sounds I heard were those present at Hare Krishna ceremonies. It was somewhat unsettling to think of having heard this music on the streets of American cities, the same music that was performed in accompaniment to this vile dancing program.

As I looked up I saw the transvestite dancer twirling and drawing near to where we stood. Faster and faster he spinned until suddenly he stopped dead in his tracks just a few feet in front of us. He paused for a moment and stared us straight in the eye. It was a knowing look as if to say, "You're not fooling me. I realize that you are here for more than simple purposes of observation."

My wife tensely gripped my arm and whispered in my ear, "There is no question about it, you can see demon powers in his eyes. It's frightening."

I reassuringly put my arm about her and walked away a few paces. Turning to one of the men standing there I asked, "What is this homosexual doing at what is supposed to be a religious function? In our religion, Christianity, this man is condemned and the Bible says that he cannot enter into heaven."

The man looked at me somewhat bewildered and replied, "In our religion he is worse than an animal. We look upon him as no better than a beggar, but this is what the people want for entertainment and so this is what we let them have."

"What a feeble excuse," I thought to myself. Yet there seemed something appropriate about such a perverted display of entertainment to accompany a depraved religious ritual.

We left the men to their dancing and walked near the pit. I began to converse with one of the men standing near and learned that he was the temple manager. We talked as I watched the ceremony taking place.

The priest was bowing again and again in front of the idol and saying prayers to the various Hindu gods. They wanted to be certain they had all the help they could get, and so he invoked the help of scores of Hindu deities. The devotees were sitting in the pit itself saying prayers. I asked if I

169

could take a closeup picture of the idol from the center of the pit. The manager indicated that it would be all right, but I would have to first take off my shoes and belt. These are made of leather and, since they worship the cow, if I didn't remove them I would be desecrating their holy grounds. I consented and stepped to the middle of the pit for my photograph. As I stood there it seemed hard to believe that on that same spot, in twenty-four hours, demon-possessed Hindus would be walking on flaming coals.

I talked further with the temple priest about the ceremony. "What contribution does the fire-walk make to the religious environment of your community?" I inquired.

"The fire-walk provides an atmosphere for the Hindus to see the existence of God's power. Then they won't do bad things. A religious function like this makes people be good," he answered.

"What do you think about the torturing aspects of the ceremony?" I asked. "I understand that they are going to drive spikes through the cheeks of the fire-walkers before they step on to the coals."

He answered that he didn't like the idea of the spikes but that it could have some good teaching. "It shows us that we can do anything by praying to our gods. That's a lesson everybody should learn," he explained.

I saw that the prayer was getting more intense. "They are getting ready to light the fire," the manager informed me. "Sometimes the power of God is so strong that fire comes from the sky and the logs light themselves," he explained.

I wasn't sure whether or not this was a true story or just a matter of superstition. It could be

170

possible, I reasoned to myself, but Satan's power was certainly limited the day that Elijah called down fire from heaven.

The devotees began to laboriously drag the logs into the pit and stacked them into a conical shape. They were building their own bonfire. What an exaggerated application of our saying about a man "digging his own grave." In this instance they are the ones who start the flames they will walk on the following night.

When the firewood was constructed appropriately it was set afire. The tongues of flame leaped up three to four feet into the sky as the devotees stared upon the face of the idol with intense devotion.

I had seen enough for this night. Now there would be just the waiting for the actual fire-walk itself. As I walked away from the pit area with heat from the firewood warming my back, I listened to the whine of a jet engine overhead as the plane approached the landing site of the tourist airport some miles away. It seemed in direct contrast to the scene about me. How tragic that in such a technologically progressive era when men can streak through the skies at hundreds of miles per hour, these devotees should kneel in worship to an inanimate wooden idol. I had no condemnation for these Hindu devotees. What they did, they did in religious ignorance. How sad that in so-called Christian America there are those who just as readily bow before their gods of lust, materialism, and pleasure. They too are blinded, though they would consider themselves educated and enlightened. I bedded down that night with anticipation for the next day's event,

171

not knowing that on the morrow I would face one of the strangest encounters of my life.

The next morning I was awakened early by a knock at the door.

"A Mr. Singh is downstairs and wants to see you," the hotel clerk informed me. Mr. Singh!—the instrument of Satan to interrupt my witnessing two days earlier. As I thought back on how he had prevented my going beyond the resurrection of Christ, I was even more convinced that he was now wanting to hinder my intentions of that day. I was certain that once again he was being sent to harass me.

I put on my clothes and walked downstairs to see him. He kindly suggested that he would like to show us around the island for the day. I firmly declined and went back upstairs to rest some more.

About noon we decided to get something to eat in the hotel restaurant. I had just begun my meal when Mr. Singh walked in the door again. I did not want to antagonize him since I couln't be sure how much he was consciously promoting Satan's purposes, so I invited him to sit and have a cup of tea with us. He had been seated only a few moments when I abruptly became violently ill. I didn't realize at that time what had come over me.

Turning to my wife I said, "Kathy, I don't understand it but all of a sudden I am extremely ill. Please excuse me. I am going to have to run up to the room."

I rushed upstairs and vomited until my stomach heaved convulsively. Afterwards, I collapsed on the bed and and was to remain there the rest of the afternoon.

As each hour grew on I became progressively more ill. I realized that unless there was a dramatic improvement in my condition there was absolutely no way I would be able to attend the fire-walk. Time after time I prayed asking the Lord to touch my body and take away the nausea. All my prayers seemed to avail nothing. Glancing at the clock I recognized that if I were going to the fire-walk, I would have to leave before six o'clock.

At five o'clock I asked my wife to go downstairs and get some food. "Just get some fish," I said. "That should be easy to chew, and with some soup I might be able to hold it down."

She returned a few minutes later. I struggled to eat what she had brought, but a couple of bites later it all came back up. I'll never forget the frustrated hopelessness that gripped me as I lay down across the bed. In desperation I cried out to God, "Lord, there is only one way now for me to get up off of this bed and go to that fire-walk. You are going to have to touch my body!"

As I began to seek God I realized that what I was experiencing was not a natural illness. I had been the victim of an oppressive attack of Satan. On various occasions I had heard ministers and missionaries speak of being satanically oppressed, but I do not know that I had ever been consciously aware of experiencing it in my own life until that time. As I thought back upon the day I recognized that I had been feeling perfectly well until Mr. Singh sat down beside me. When correlating this with the experience two nights before, I came to the conclusion that Mr. Singh was the instrument to bring about this attack of the enemy.

With this realization in mind I began to take

authority in the name of Jesus. I cried out, "Dear Jesus, this thing that has attacked my body is a spirit of Satan. In the name of Jesus I command that it leave me and that I be restored to perfect health."

I cannot describe the feeling that came over my body and the buoyancy that I experienced in my spirit. Instantaneously my headache and nausea were gone. I leaped to my feet and began to walk about the room thanking God for his miraculous intervention. "Kathy," I shouted, "go get the clerk and tell him to have a taxi ready. I am going to the fire-walk!"

We got in the car and began our journey to the temple. Back in the motel room before the Lord touched my body, I had asked Kathy to get some aspirins for me. We were halfway to the fire-walk when I realized she had never brought me the aspirins. "I am glad you didn't bring them," I said to her. "Now I won't be tempted to trust in flesh. I will depend upon God to keep my body well."

As we drove to the fire-walk I searched my mind for an explanation as to why God had permitted the demonic attack upon my body. I do not believe, as some teach, that a Christian can be demonically possessed. The spirit of Satan and the spirit of God can not dwell in the same vessel. I do believe that it is possible for Christians to experience oppression, especially when they are not in a right relationship with the Lord. Why, then, had God permitted by body to become afflicted?

As I reminisced on what had taken place in the last several days one thing stood out in my mind: there seemed to be an overwhelming preoccupation with the supernatural powers of Satan. I had constantly been shocked to see his ability to enslave these people through such phenomena. Perhaps God needed to show me that He who is in me is greater than he who is without me. God had placed me in a position where I realized that without His hand of protection on my life, Satan could at will attack my being. By His instantaneous defeat of the powers that oppressed me, the Lord was showing that He was the mightier, lest I become too impressed with the workings of Satan.

As I look back now I wonder, if God hadn't taken me through this experience, if I might have been tempted to fear rather than respect the power of Satan. This I know for certain: that night on the way to the fire-walk, my thoughts were not about the satanic ritual I was going to observe. As we rode along I sang gospel choruses and intermittently stopped to praise and thank God for his wonderful love. My constant focus was upon the reality of Christ in my life and His power to defeat our adversary, the devil.

When we arrived at the firewalk area I was amazed to see that the fifteen tons of firewood had been reduced to a small pile of flaming coals. One of the temple assistants was stoking the coals as fire leaped from them. I had no sooner walked up to the pit and prepared my camera for photography than the action began.

I heard the sound of drums and out of nowhere the fire-walking devotees emerged in single file. To the rhythm of the savage drumbeat they danced around and around the pit in a processional. I had been allowed inside of the roped-off area because I had told them I would write a book on what I was going to observe. (If only they could read this book now.) The Indian Hindu observers were restricted to the nonholy area outside of the ropes. As I maneuvered for some close-up shots the temple manager came near and warned me to be careful. "At times they become quite violent and go into seizures," he explained.

I inquired as to why they danced to the music. He explained that it helped them to become spirited. I listened as the beat pounded over and over and over again. It was quite obvious to me that the primitive nature of the rhythm was very much akin to that which is commonly associated with the harder styles of rock music. To an untrained ear it perhaps sounded slightly cacophonous, but to my ear I detected a very intricate form of pulsated syncopation.

Turning to the manager I commented, "You know, that beat sounds a lot like what one hears in rock-and-roll music."

He laughed slightly. "Yes, it is quite similar, isn't it?"

"Is there anything you can tell me about these rhythms?" I asked.

"Well," he said, "these are the same ones that we have used for centuries. Some people have tried to get us to change them but we have found these rhythms to be the most effective to get us into the conditions so our gods may possess us."

Startled at his answer, I asked somewhat facetiously, "Maybe you'd like to have the Rolling Stones play at your next fire-walk?"

"Oh, no!" he replied somewhat indignantly. "That would not be appropriate. This is a religious function and you certainly wouldn't

176

want a rock-and roll band to play at something religious, would you?"

Those who are familiar with my previous writings can imagine what went through my mind at that point. How strange it is that this pagan heathen had more respect for spiritual things than some pastors and youth leaders in America! He at least had enough spiritual sensitivity to recognize that rock-and-roll music would not be appropriate for anything religious. What an indictment it is of those who suggest that this music can be used of God and blessed by the Holy Spirit. The volume on occult history, *Magic and the Supernatural,* (copyright 1964, published 1970 by Hamlyn Publishing Group Ltd., New York) speaks on page 178 of voodoo dancers who "are capable of making convulsive movements for hours on end to rhythms which would give anyone who was not in their 'second state' a heart attack. The same is probably true to some extent of rock 'n' roll dancers."

As they continued their dancing they became ever more violent and frenzied. Pieces of burning camphor had been placed strategically about the fire-pit area and provided the only light. As the flames and smoke reached skyward it lent an aura of satanic strangeness to the whole situation.

Finally, the dancing was concluded and the devotees stripped to the waist. The priest came and placed a ring of flowers about each of their necks. It was quite apparent that as a result of their dancing a change had come over them. The temple manager had stated that the dancing helped them to get into the position to become spirit-possessed. As I looked at their eyes I began to see exactly what he meant.

I asked if I could get them to pose for a group picture. He spoke with them and they consented. They knelt by the side of the pit, permitting me to take several photographs. As I stared into their eyes they seemed to look right through me. They were glazed over as if in a trance.

One of the young lads I was photographing was the son of the temple manager. His father had explained to me the purpose for which the boy was walking on the fire. A year before the child had become somewhat incorrigible. He began drinking, smoking, and running with the wrong crowd. He also neglected his studies, and his father became quite concerned. Then one day the temple priest asked if the father would allow his son to walk on the fire. At first he said no. After much coaxing from the priest, he finally consented to allow his son to walk. The temple manager slowingly related this story: "My son's whole life literally changed; he quit smoking, drinking, and began to attend school with his grades improving. Now," the manager said, "I believe in the fire-walk."

One point here is worthy of consideration. Moral transformation is no proof in itself of the gospel of Jesus Christ. Other religions possess the power to change men morally. To suggest that subjective testimonies of conversion validate the gospel can be to place the life in Christ on an ethical par with other religious faiths. Let us always understand that the ultimate substantiation of the truth of the gospel rests on the claims of Christ and the written revelation of God's Word.

I thanked the devotees for allowing me to take their picture, but I am not sure they heard. In fact I am not sure they were aware of anything that was going on about them. They were already in a semitrance state and were like satanic zombie-robots.

The temple manager walked over to me and began to converse again. "Are you enjoying the ceremony thus far?" he asked.

I did not reply in the affirmative but merely offered an ambiguous comment on the whole scene.

"When you get back to America," he said, "please tell the people there about what you have seen. We would very much like to bring the fire-walk to America. If someone would just pay our expenses we would come with no charges. Wouldn't it be wonderful if the fire-walk could be portrayed before a group of your young people? I am sure they would be very interested."

I had to assent that the feat would doubtless fascinate them, but I could not agree that it would be a wonderful thing to do. I assured him that I would tell the young people in America about his request, but I did not say that I would do everything within my power to prevent it. America has had enough damage done from the self-styled spiritual gurus of the East. I would not want to be one to further aid Satan's efforts.

It appeared as if the ceremony were drawing to a conclusion. The priest walked to the altar prepared in front of the idol and took a whip in his hands. I asked the temple manager what that was about. He explained that after they were done with the preparatory rituals they would then walk one-half mile down to the river. There they would cleanse in the water as a final act of purification. With the whip the priest would flagellate each of them. I couldn't help but think of Christ who was beaten for us. I was saddened too, knowing that no amount of water could ever wash away their sins. It is the blood Jesus shed as He suffered for us that alone can cleanse a man from sin.

The priest took a pan of burning camphor and knelt in front of the idol offering fire to it. The Hindus believe that Draupati, their goddess, was born in the fire and that is why they believe she has the power to keep them from being burned.

In a final gesture of submission the priest and devotees knelt before the idol chanting their final petition for power to walk on the fire. Just before departing for the river they stopped at the pit, standing before it with hands clasped in a gesture of prayer. Then, in single file, they began their journey.

It was approximately forty-five minutes before they returned for the fire-walk. During this time I wandered about the pit area inspecting the surroundings. One of the assistants began to level off the pile of coals and spread them out to a uniform depth in the pit. I can give personal testimony as to the reality of the fire. The heat was so intense that whenever I would try to approach the pit any closer than five feet, the searing flames were unbearable. It was hard to believe that in spite of the fact I could not approach safely within a few steps of the pit, the fire-walkers were actually going to step on these flaming, red-hot coals.

Suddenly I heard screams in the distance. As the sound drew nearer I could see the fire-walkers.

The sound was coming from the intensity of their demonic frenzy. Suddenly they burst into the pit area marching around and around single file. Then they stopped directly in front of the pit. Wanting to get close-ups with my camera, I approached within a few feet of the fire-walkers. They were not the same men I had seen a few moments before. Their eyes had a hellish fury in them and there could be no mistaking that they were now totally dominated by demon spirits.

In final preparation the priest was handed a quantity of six-inch-long, knife-like spikes. One by one he pierced the tongues and cheeks of the devotees, leaving the spikes inserted as part of their devotional. They breathed heavily, foamed at the mouth, and writhed and screamed in a manner that can only be described as coming from satanic inspiration.

The priest then walked to the idol and lifted the garland of flowers that was sitting on its head. This was the same garland that had been used for the supernatural levitation phenomenon associated with the prayers of the devotees. He strode to the front of the pit and methodically cast the flowers into the flames—they did not burn! I could scarcely believe my eyes. The flowers lay in the midst of the hottest coals and yet did not so much as wilt. Then, as casually as one would stroll down the street, with brisk steps the priest stepped out onto the flames. He explained to me later that he had to go through the fire first to show his followers an example of trust in the power of the idol.

With a new surge of satanic faith running through their bodies, the devotees screamed and

181

shouted as if begging for their opportunity to step into the flames. Then they came. At first they walked through as a unit, some of them dancing and prancing to the beat of the accompanying music. Next they walked one by one, each in his turn, across the twenty-foot pathway of white-hot coals. Some of them danced and gyrated wildly, while others walked through calmly. Those who strode nonchalantly were apparently wanting to give evidence of their complete faith in the power of the gods.

Among those walking through was a woman who had done so several times. Her faith was so strong, according to the Hindus, that she did not even have to go to the river for the purification process. She had been through the pit so often that she could easily yield herself to the power of the gods.

All the while they walked through the pit I could see the garland lying there unharmed in the flames. One devotee stood perfectly still for a few moments in the flames. He bowed slowly three times at the idol and then picked up the coals in his hands. He smiled as if to give further proof that he had complete trust in the power of the gods to keep him from blistering. Then he piled the coals on the top of his head—not one hair was singed. Again and again they walked through the fire, each devotee making about eight to ten trips. I started to count the number of trips across the coals but it all happened so fast I just lost track. After about fifteen minutes of fire-walking it was all over.

One of the young fire-walkers walked over to the idol of the goddess and picked it up in his

182

arms. He carried it about, dancing and praising the power of Draupati. I looked at the eyes of the idol and then at the eyes of the young man. It was then that I realized why the eyes of the idol were depicted in the enlarged, intensely staring manner. It was just the same way that the eyes of the fire-walkers looked. They did not appear that way when I had seen them the night before. It was after the dancing processional that the spirit had entered into them and transformed their appearance as well as their lives.

As abruptly as it began, the fire-walking was concluded. The priest dipped a branch into a pail of holy water and sprinkled it about the coals, signifying the end of the fire-walk. I mingled about the devotees, talking with them and inquiring as to their thoughts regarding what they had just undergone. The youngest lad to walk held in his hands the spikes that had been piercing their cheeks. He smiled, as friendly and cheery as one would expect a small child to be. It just seemed hard to believe that only minutes before demonic forces had completely controlled his life.

The walkers were anxious for me to see their feet, and they sat on the grass holding up their soles. They did not even have the smell of smoke and no sign of a blister.

The women who had sponsored the fire-walk were obviously elated at such a successful venture. They sat down in a circle to clap their hands, sing, pray, and beat on the drums. When I asked the temple manager what was taking place he explained that they were now singing praises of thankfulness to the gods for such a successful manifestation of their power. I thought of the many times that God had answered prayer in my life and how I had neglected being sufficiently thankful. What a rebuke it is to followers of Christ to know that many times the heathen who ignorantly worship the devil are more thankful than we who accept the free gift of salvation through Jesus Christ.

Some of the young devotees walked over to the dormitory area where food was being served. They hadn't eaten for a week and were obviously starved. They shoveled it in vigorously.

I walked back over near the pit and talked with the temple manager for a few final minutes. Standing near the coals, I still could not approach too closely because of the intense heat, even though this was many minutes after the devotees had walked on the coals. The manager told me that the area in which I was now standing was holy and sanctified unto the goddess.

I had him introduce me to the priest who had directed the fire-walking and conversed through an interpreter. His answers to my questions were most revealing. He said that he had never received any scars or any injury at all. I asked his age and he replied that he was fifty-six. When I inquired as to how long he would continue fire-walking he simply replied, "As long as I'm able to walk."

As I think back on all of it now it is still difficult to believe that what I saw actually took place. Why do they walk on the fire? The answer lies much deeper than their explanation, "to display the power of our goddess." In a certain sense they are right. There are two forces at work in this world: the power of Christ who died to redeem men from their sins and the power of Satan who desires to enslave men in bondage and eventual destruction. Regretfully the god worshiped by these sincere and devoted people is none other than Satan. It is the power of demons that enables them to undergo this supernatural feat.

I know that hypnosis and trance states could be used as an explanation for what took place. But such a condition would serve only to protect them from pain. It could never protect them from being burned or even having the slightest smell of smoke. A spiritual explanation is the only logical conclusion. The devil is basically an imitator of God. He always tries to counterfeit every miracle spoken of in the Bible. It seems that he cannot complacently sit by and allow God to have the upper hand without challenge. So by an infusion of his power into men he seeks to accomplish a mimicry of the power of the true God.

As God protected the three Hebrew children, so it is that Satan seeks a similar manifestation of his power. He wants to boast that he too has this ability. Unfortunately it is the power of hell. In Isaiah 43:2 we read, "When you walk through the fire you shall not be burned, the flames shall not consume you." This is the promise of God's Word and what I have just described is an attempt of Satan to duplicate that Scripture.

In spite of the evident power of Satan, he does have a limitation. The three Hebrew children did not just walk on coals; their whole bodies were surrounded in flames but God protected them. When I asked the priest how long they could walk in the fire, he said not more than fifteen minutes. Perhaps, he said, they could walk for an hour but it would take much more fasting and prayer. One of the fire-walkers said that he was in a total trance every time through the pit except the last trip where he began to sense what was happening. My point is this: Satan's power is limited.

I am reminded of Daniel, who prayed to God in spite of the command of the authorities. It was all night, not an hour or ten minutes, that he stayed in the lions' den. Even though Satan has great abilities, he can only work within a limited sphere in which God yet tolerates him to act.

Perhaps one might ask, "Could Christ protect someone who walked through the flames to prove His power?" The answer is undeniably yes, but as to whether or not one should walk upon the fire presumptuously to prove God's power, that is another matter. Our duty as Christians is to trust in God. No matter what dangers may confront us we have the assurance that nothing shall befall us but that Christ shall protect and preserve us. To presume upon His power and seek to display it for self-pride or egotistical honor is to tempt God. We are not to assume that we may deliberately place ourselves in danger and that God is obligated to protect us. We must trust in Him, knowing that He orders our each step. Should our pathway take us through the fire, God will protect us. But let us not presume that we can walk into adversity deliberately. God is not then obligated to preserve us.

Satan demands that his followers openly place their lives in danger in order to prove their devotion. He then protects them from these adversities, but the price is a big one. In return they are automatically enslaved to do his bidding and are dominated by his power. In contrast, the

186

gospel declares that men can do nothing to please God. There is no way that we may merit the gift of salvation. It is not for us to prove devotion by deliberately endangering our bodies. Rather, we are implored to present our bodies as a "living sacrifice unto God." In return, we receive the free gift of eternal life through Jesus Christ. To whom have you yielded your life, the god of hellfire or the Christ of Calvary?

8

Finders Keepers

One of the criticisms of many current books dealing with demonism is that those which include personal encounters invariably strike only a positive note. The impression is sometimes given that every episode of spiritistic possession concludes with the battle being won over the powers of darkness. One would thus be led to believe that the war against satanic forces is being won overwhelmingly in favor of the Kingdom of God.

Certainly those who encounter occult subjection should not be faulted for wanting to give a positive testimony. The Christian emphasis should primarily be on the overcoming power of the Gospel with minor attention given to the enslaving abilities of Satan. The readers of this and other Christian books on the occult should realize that Christ who is in us is greater than he who is in the world. Through the power in the name of Jesus we have total dominance over Satan's legions. Still there is some validity in the argument that presenting only that side of the story can give a lopsided view of the total picture. Scripture does show through the words of Jesus (Matthew 7:13,14) that the majority of people will not choose to follow Christ. Only a small minority will inherit the Kingdom of God and most will follow the ways of Satan. In terms of numbers of adherents, it is questionable whether or not the majority of people in occultism are being delivered from such satanic bondage. Unfortunately, it appears as though Satan is temporarily winning the day, even though we know he will eventually be defeated by Christ.

I cannot pass judgment on other writers or ministers who have dealt in the area of the occult. It may well be that there are some of them who have experienced only complete victory in the lives of those whom they have counseled, but I rather doubt this is the case. Candidly, some authors may have done a disservice to the credibility of exorcism by failing to tell the other side of the picture.

As Christians we must always be willing to be honest and tell the whole truth. It may not sound exciting to our listeners and readers to hear stories of satanic victory, but we must be totally frank in relating that side of the story as well. It is with this thought in mind that I share with you the following encounter. The story of Marcia will also point out the seriousness of this whole subject of satanism. The devil is playing for keeps and he means business. He is not to be feared but to be respected as the second power of this universe, capable of imprisoning lives in the most horrible acts of depravity.

Before describing our encounter with ritualistic human sacrifices, it might be well to point out that this phenomenon has an ancient history in not only the black arts but pagan worship as well. It is a well-known fact that the Indians of pre-Columbian Mexico practiced human sacrifices on their altar to the corn goddess. It was customary to slit the chest of the victim and present the heart to the deity. So serious was this form of Satan worship that at times its toll ran into thousands of lives. When the followers of Cortez explored the Grand Temple of Mexico they found the skulls of the human sacrifice victims. One soldier claimed to have counted 136,000 of them. But the Mexicans were not alone.

The Druids also practiced ritual murder in a form approximating that of the Mexican sacrifices. The spiritual purpose of such deeds was often to make the victim a scapegoat for the mistakes and difficulties of the community. This, of course, is a satanic counterfeit to the Jewish scapegoat of the Old Testament upon which the sins of the people were laid. The pagan civilizations of Old Testament times were infamous for their worship of Moloch. This was one of the deities referred to in Deuteronomy 18, where the Lord commanded the Israelites not to allow any of their children to "pass through the fire." Incineration of children was particularly prevalent among the Ammonites. This gruesome orgy was carried out by placing the body of the live child into the arms of the large idol which had been hollowed out and a roaring fire built inside. Such practices took place among the Canaanites as late as the seventh century B.C.

Throughout history cannibalism has also been practiced as a form of demon worship. The idea in part behind this ritual is the magical conception that the forces and characteristics of the dead will be assimilated in the bodies of the consumer. One of the most horrid examples in modern times is the fifteenth-century account of Gilles de Laval, Baron de Retz. Gilles, who according to historians was possessed of a demon, sacrificed innumerable children. His story was recounted in Berrault's *Bluebeard*.

During the middle ages this black art reached an apex and the sacrifice of children became commonplace. Stillborn babies and unbaptized infants were especially sought after for cannibalistic purposes. All across Europe many witches became midwives and dedicated babies to Satan the instant they were born. To counteract this the Roman Catholic church even formed a society of male midwives to baptize infants before the severance of the umbilical cord. So great in demand were such sacrifices that witches who were unable to produce a child of their own had to procure one by some other means such as kidnaping. Many old engravings and fabled accounts speak of children being presented to the devil to receive his mark on their body. Perhaps even more grisly is the account of witches using the corpses of children to make fat for their ointments and candles.

Twentieth-century examples of human sacrifice are not absent. They are particularly prevalent in satanic orders that take place in countries where murder is difficult to trace because of inept police procedures. Unimportant people in such areas who disappear frequently often become the victims of modern devil worshipers. In the impoverished and overpopulated areas of eastern Europe, Africa, and Asia, the concealment of such practices is not difficult. Who is going to miss one small child in such an area where human life is already considered extremely cheap?

In summary, a casual survey of the history of human sacrifices reveals a variety of motives. Some felt that the offering up of a human life would be the ultimate form of appeasement by which to gain the pleasure of the diety. In some instances the seriousness and the vileness of this act helped to bind together the devotees in a cult of greater cohesiveness based on the drastic measures required by this deed. Of special note from the Christian standpoint is the expiatory theory that suggests such sacrifices were a means of atoning for sin. The victim thus becomes a substitute to endure the penalty actually due to those who perform the sacrifice. One can easily see here the counterfeit and satanic distortion of the Levitical offering of the lamb without blemish and more specifically the offering up of Christ for the sins of the world.

At this point the reader may be tempted to view all I have written with a completely historical outlook. As horrible as the thought of live sacrifices is, it is possible to conceive of such rituals taking place during ancient pagan times or more recently the era of the Dark Ages. Do such things still occur today? The reader may be further inclined to accept the possibility of such unspeakable deeds performed in faraway heathen lands bound by idol worship. What about America? Can such deeds be a part of contemporary life? Are today's new occultists and satanic practioners actually offering live sacrifices as their ultimate devotion? Only the uninformed or naive would answer no.

During the invitation for conversion that I issued at the conclusion of a message during a recent crusade I noted with particular interest one of those who was responding, a teen-age girl who was obviously distraught. As she walked down the aisle toward the altar where I waited, she did so with faltering and hesitant steps. She seemed to be staggering as if in some type of stupor, taking two steps forward and then stepping back a pace or two. As she progressed, grabbing the ends of the pews to steady herself, I wondered if perhaps she might be drunk or under the influence of drugs. It would not be the first time I have had a young person respond to Christ while in a dope-induced state, later to be sobered by the Holy Spirit. But the look on the face of this teen-ager spoke of such anguish and torment that it soon became apparent she was experiencing more than a flashback or hallucination. Finally, she reached the altar and collapsed on the floor at my feet. I asked several counselors to escort her away. Since the invitation was not concluded, I requested that they deal with her further in prayer while I returned to extend the appeal.

At the conclusion of the service I proceeded to

193

counsel with those who were seeking personal attention for spiritual needs. I was so busy that I had forgotten the young lady just described. On this particular evening several hours were spent with those who came seeking guidance. After I had talked with what I thought was the last person and was preparing to leave the sanctuary, I noticed Marcia standing near the platform. She called out to me, and when I approached her she began to plead, "Please, Mr. Larson, you've got to help me. I'm in trouble and I need God."

I assumed she had not received adequate counseling for her need and requested that my wife and one of the pastors accompany me to the prayer room for further inquiry. Her openness and desperation of pleading seemed to subside once we reached the counseling room. She almost immediately began to insist that perhaps she really didn't need all that much help and that we should leave her alone. Regaining her composure, she insisted that everything was all right and that she had worked out the problem in her own mind to satisfaction. I was convinced that this was not the case and suspected that she was trying to rationalize whatever was troubling her.

I probed her for some time, asking every question that I felt was pertinent but she failed to divulge anything that would be helpful in going further with the counseling. The more we spoke the more incoherent she became. Her speech began to ramble indiscriminately and communication grew increasingly difficult. We tried to get her to pray, but at first she refused. I knew there was no way we could help her unless she was willing to open up and tell us what the real problem was.

Finally she agreed to have prayer with us. She refused to pray on her own, but did consent to repeat words after me. As I began to voice the prayer she followed word by word until I came to the name of Jesus. At that point she gagged as if vomiting and complained of a choking sensation at her throat. An extreme sense of fatigue came over her and she slumped to the floor, complaining of not being able to stay awake. "Leave me alone," she demanded, "I'm tired and I want to rest. Don't bother me, just let me be so that I can sleep."

Though I had remotely suspected demonic influence in the beginning, my policy in such a situation is not to suggest that diagnosis until all other avenues have been exhausted. Now that she found it impossible to repeat the name of Jesus and had abruptly experienced an unnatural tiredness, my suspicions grew stronger.

I kept insisting that she stay awake and when she tried to slump to the floor would help her to her feet to be seated again. Her mood gradually changed from indifference and lethargy to one of agressive hysteria and her voice grew louder and more hostile. Suddenly, she jumped to her feet and began to march frantically about the room at a near run. Back and forth she paced from one end to the other. With an increasing incoherence of speech she began to bang her head against the wall crying out, "It's no use. You can't help me. There's no way out. Leave me alone."

At first we tried restraint and told her that if she did not quit beating her head that she could inflict dangerous injury. She refused to heed our pleas and only became more violent in her reactions. We let this go on for a few moments until the sense of fatigue once again overcame her.

At this point I wanted to make one final confirmation before concluding that demonism was in actuality what we were facing. I stepped outside of the counseling room for a moment to speak with several of her girlfriends who were waiting there for her. The young lady who had brought her to the service that evening was the one I spoke with first.

"We're having some difficulties in counseling with Marcia," I informed her. "How long have you known her?"

"I guess I've known her all my life," was the answer. "Why? What's wrong?"

I explained in part what was happening. "Has Marcia ever exhibited any extremely aggressive, irrational, or chaotic emotional behavior?" I asked.

The girls laughed slightly and Marcia's best friend answered, "Of course not. She's just as normal as you and me. There's nothing wrong with her. Why? What's going on in there?"

I did not want to publicly broadcast what I felt was a very personal, private counseling session. "I'd rather not tell you the whole story," I answered. "All I can say is that it is a very serious matter. Just pray!"

I stepped back into the counseling room determined to deal with this matter head-on. "Marcia, I'm going to ask you some questions that I want you to truthfully answer. Don't lie to me or it could be dangerous."

While I had been outside, she had somewhat calmed down. A serious look came over her face, undoubtedly a demonic influence, as Satan knew that a showdown was coming. "Have you ever made a pact of any kind with the devil?" I demanded to know.

With that, she jumped to her feet and began to hysterically run about the room screaming, "My God, my God, it was only a baby. Its body was still warm. I saw it move. I know it was alive. My God, it was only a baby."

"What do you mean, Marcia? What are you talking about? What did you do with the baby?" I inquired.

She either was refusing to answer my question or was so overcome with emotion that she was incapable of replying. I tried to calm her and continued to insist that she tell me what she was raving about.

"My God, my God, it was only a baby!" she screamed over and over again.

"What did you do with the baby?" I asked.

"I burned it alive on an altar to Satan!" was the startling answer.

I must confess that in spite of my many dealings with occultism and direct encounters with Satanism in its rawest forms, even I was stunned. My wife and the pastor stared with the same incredulous look on their faces. How could what she was saying be true, here in Christian America, in such a supposedly progressive age? Was this girl only mentally ill with horrible delusions of misdeeds? I had no reason to assume that this was the case. This dramatic revelation had taken place only when I demanded to know of her satanic involvement, if any.

"Where did you get the baby?" I inquired further.

By now the hysteria had subsided and a sense of futile despair had overtaken her. She went limp and collapsed to the floor, just staring out into space. "The mother had the baby for the devil and she gave it to us," was the answer.

"What did you do with the mother after the child was sacrificed?" I wanted to know.

"We told her that if she wanted to be happy she would have to join the baby. Then we gave her a knife and instructed her to cut her body with it. She did, until she bled to death. Then we put her on the altar and burned her too!"

I was shocked even more. Not just one murder but two lives taken in the name of worship to Satan. In a disbelieving tone of voice I asked, "How could you do such a thing? What was happening while she cut herself?"

Marcia slightly shrugged her shoulders and a pathetic half-grin came across her lips. "Oh, that's easy," she answered. "We sat around her in a circle and held hands singing Christian hymns just like you sang tonight."

At that prospect my blood chilled. I looked at my wife who, by this time, was almost literally, physically ill.

"Does anybody else know about this?" I inquired.

"Just Dan and the others who are part of our group," she answered. I asked who Dan was, as this was the first time he had been brought into the picture. "Dan is our leader," I was informed. "He loves me and I love him. He tells us what to do and we do it. You know," she went on, "what I did seems so horrible now but at the time it wasn't so bad. It never seems bad. Dan gives us some green stuff to drink and when we do, I don't know, everything just seems right. I can do anything when I drink that stuff Dan gives me. Nothing matters after that."

"How did all of this get started?" I wanted to know. "Where did you ever get involved with this group of Satan worshipers?"

The story that followed depicted an occult pattern to which I was not foreign. Marcia told how as a child she became ill with rheumatic fever and was permanently confined to bed. Her case was so bad that her parents feared she might be disabled for life. One day a man came to the front door. No one knew who he was, but he told Marcia's mother that he was aware there was a sick child in the house and that he had the power to heal her. Marcia explained that they thought he must somehow have been an angel of God sent to help them. The man at the door, it turned out, was Dan's father. As Marcia desribed the manner in which he prayed over her it was a typical description of mediumistic-style healing procedures. This, incidently, was the first time that she had ever seen Dan, though he was just a small child at the time. After the man left, her parents noted a remarkable improvement in her condition and in a short time the illness was completely gone.

I would at this point like to interject that I am in no way condemning true servants of God, be they pastors or cvangelists, who have experienced dramatic instances of healing and recovery after prayer. We are, after all, admonished in James chapter five to pray for the sick. The Word declares that "the prayer of faith shall save the sick, and the Lord shall raise him up" (James 5:15). It is wrong to ignore or omit such teachings simply because this practice has often been misused by the unscrupulous and sensationalized tactics of some so-called healing evangelists. At the same time I wish to point out that healing practices are an ancient as well as present-day form of occult attachment. In some instances the illness has been satanically induced through oppression, only to be relieved by Satan himself at the price of later demonic enslavement. The ancient Egyptians were adept in the occult healing arts. The tribal medicine man known in African, East Indian, and North American folklore was in reality a trafficker in demonism. Even today, spiritualist mediums claim healing power and some such as Edgar Cayce have been able to effect seemingly remarkable cures.

The healings encounter was the last time Marcia had seen Dan until later as a teen-ager. It was then that they became romantically involved. Whenever a mediumistic healing takes place, the disorder is often transferred from the physical to the psychic level. In this case, Marcia had been "healed" at the price of later selling her life out to satanic worship.

I questioned then and do now whether or not Dan was really in love with Marcia. In her telling of the story it was quite obvious that he manipulated her for his own personal and selfish desires. It is probable that he only fed her a line about

loving her to get her in a position to do his bid-
dings, whether for personal gratification or satanic ends. Whatever the case may have been,
she followed Dan to do whatever he asked without
question, even to the extent of a live, human sacrifice. It was obvious that the mediumistic abilities of Dan's father had been hereditarily passed
on to him. This, too, is often the case. The
occult subjection that took place between Marcia
and Dan's father was also a spiritualistic heri-
age passed on. This as well is a pattern prevalent
in occult circles.

As Marcia shared more details regarding her
life it became apparent that her satanic involvement did not come about as the result of any
malevolent intent on her part. She had been the
pathetic tool of forces that had sought in many
ways to destroy her life. This was more obvious as
I learned of the relationship with her parents.

"Tonight is my sixteenth birthday," she said
with only a half-smile on her face. "It's supposed
to be such a great day in my life but I doubt if my
father will even show up. He and mom don't get
along too well and he is gone most of the time. He
might come home, but even if he does, he won't
show me any attention. He'll just give me some
money and tell me to go out and buy myself some
dresses," she stated somewhat sarcastically.
"I've got all the clothes I need. I don't need any
money from him. Why doesn't he just love me?
He doesn't care about me. Nobody does, just
Dan!"

What she told further about her father was even
more appalling. He was a professional drug
pusher. In fact, Marcia revealed that she was on

201

drugs herself. "My dad gives the dope to me," she explained. "He says that he loves me and that's why he keeps me on dope. It isn't love. I don't know why he does it. He pushes dope to all my friends at school. Everybody knows what my dad does. How can he say that he loves me and then turn all my friends on to drugs? He says that drugs will help me get through life and ease my emotions and pain. I don't want his money or his dope. I just want him. I wish he loved me."

As she spoke in short, choppy sentences, uttering in turn hate and hopelessness, I wept inside. I must admit that within my own being rose up a feeling of intense hatred for this man who had so cruelly helped to destroy his daughter's life. I fought back vengeance in my heart as I realized that he too was just another sinner in need of God's grace. I glanced at my wife, who was fighting to hold back tears. "My God," I thought to myself. "How could such a man dare to call himself a father and have the audacity to say that he loves his child?"

We let Marcia talk herself out. She didn't cry or weep over her situation. She just spoke softly in tones of utter desperation.

When she was finished describing everything that was pertinent regarding her background and satanic involvement, we began the counseling procedure in earnest. First I prayed, rebuking in the name of Jesus the demonic forces that had enslaved her life. I was confident that she had not been demon-possessed. There was no need for it. She was a willing instrument of Satan and he had no need to totally possess her volition. As we prayed I felt the breaking of occult chains that had bound her. Then we led her through the scriptural plan of salvation for her life. She expressed a desire to know Christ and to surrender to Him as Lord. As we prayed with her, this time, she spoke the name of Jesus easily. But, even as we prayed, questions came up again.

At this point the matter of gravest concern was the child. "What happened to the baby that we burned? Is the baby in Hell? Where did the baby go—can you tell me?"

We assured her that the child was with God.

"But we dedicated and sacrificed the baby to the devil. We told the devil that he could have the baby. How can I be sure that the baby isn't with Satan now?" she insisted upon knowing.

To calm her fears we explained the biblical position regarding the death of children. "Until a child reaches the age of accountability, an age at which it has the ability to choose between right and wrong," I explained, "God does not hold that child responsible for its inherited sinful nature through the fall of Adam and Eve. Once a person passes the age of accountability, God holds him personally responsible for his deeds and acceptance or rejection of Christ. But until that age, a child who dies before knowing right and wrong goes to be with God."

It was not an easy matter to convince her of this. Satan tried to overwhelm her with a sense of grief at her deed and was nearly successful in convincing her that he indeed had the child in his clutches. God's Word is powerful, though, and after scriptural counsel her fears were eased.

Still, one other question plagued her. "How can God ever forgive me for what I have done?" she asked. "I have committed such a horrible deed. I murdered two people and worshiped the devil. There is no way that God could ever forgive me for that. I'm lost forever!"

I have witnessed to many people about the forgiving love of Jesus Christ. I cannot say that I have ever enjoyed more sharing His great grace as I did that evening with Marcia. It is one thing to say that God can forgive to a drug addict, a prostitute, and drunkard, or even an adulterer. It is quite another to look into the face of a teen-age murderer and Satan worshiper and say, "God loves you and He can forgive you if you will ask Him to."

From memory I quoted Psalm 103:11,12. This passage of Scripture was used of the Lord to finally convince her and break the spirit of satanic guilt that clouded her thinking. Several times I repeated the words over again, "For as the heaven is high above the earth, so great is his mercy toward them that fear him. As far as the east is from the west, so far hath he removed our transgressions from us." Though it was difficult for her to accept and believe, in time we were also able to convince her on this point to the extent that she readily prayed a sinner's prayer and followed along with us as we read numerous Scriptures pertaining to salvation.

On several occasions, she would interrupt us by looking up from the Bible and quoting the scripture from memory. "I can't believe it!" she exclaimed. "I haven't heard these Scriptures since I went to a little Baptist Sunday school at seven years of age. Somehow it's all coming back to me now. I can remember what I was taught then."

We spent at least another half of an hour talking, praying and counseling with Marcia, seeking to alleviate what fears she had regarding the future. One of the most difficult tasks was to convince her that Dan did not love her and was only using her. At first she refused to believe that she had only been his selfish victim. After a time, with the help of the Lord, we were able to show her that she was his instrument to bring about diabolical intentions. She finally agreed with us on this point, which was no small victory.

We left the church rejoicing in the apparent defeat of Satan's hold upon her life. Still there were some nagging doubts in my mind. Though she had prayed a sinner's prayer and seemed to have meant it, her thinking was frequently attacked by Satan. A cloud of confusion would periodically settle in, even as we prayed. She was so desperate for love and attention that although she agreed Dan did not love her there seemed to be a vestige of attachment to him. At that point I couldn't be certain what would happen but just committed her unto the Lord and prayed that she would continue to walk in the way that we had shown her.

We gave her our address and asked that she write and stay in touch with us. She was going to be needing help, and we wanted to be available no matter what happened. It was only a few days later, after we had returned home to our office from the crusade, that we received Marcia's letter. As we began to read it, our hopes soared as she expressed her thankfulness for what God had done.

Dearest Bob and Kathy:

I just finished watching a program from your *Revelation* series on television. My parents left for a week or two. I don't know where they went. It's not the first time or the last, but I'm a big girl and I can take care of myself.

I miss you two. I feel closer to you and your wife than I have felt to anyone, even Dan. I tried to forget what you said about him not loving me but I guess that I've always known it. It's just hard to give up something that you thought you couldn't live without. I love you for showing the peace that God can give. I'll always remember you both. You made me feel alive.

Will you please write to me, especially you, Kathy, if you have time? When you smiled at me, Kathy, I knew that everything was going to be okay.

Must go. All my love.

Marcia.

At that point in reading the letter, Kathy and I smiled at one another praising the Lord inside. A moment later our spirits plunged as we read a P.S. that had been added to this same letter several days later.

P.S. I just left Dan. I can't write any more. I'm mailing this to let you know how I love you all. I am sorry I wasted your time. I met Dan on the beach today. I love to swim and this time I started swimming and my mind was blank until I stopped. I was further out than ever before. I started back but I was exhausted. I tried to float for awhile but I panicked. I started to struggle and started sinking. I thought I was going to die.

206

But Dan swam out and saved my life. I don't know what got into me! I owe my life to him. I knew all of this was too good to be true. I guess that it was just meant to be this way. No matter what's happened, as Dan reminded me, he found me and *finders keepers*.